Penguin Education

Penguin Modern Economics Texts
General Editor: B. J. McCormick

Development Economics
Editor: Peter Robson

International Trade and Economic Development
G. K. Helleiner

Penguin Modern Economics Texts
General Editor: B. J. McCormick
Senior Lecturer in Economics
University of Sheffield

Development Economics
Editor: P. Robson
Professor of Economics
St Salvator's College
University of St Andrews

Econometrics
Editor: G. R. Fisher
Professor of Econometrics
University of Southampton

Economic Thought
Editor: K. J. W. Alexander
Professor of Economics
University of Strathclyde

Industrial Economics
Editor: H. Townsend
Reader in Economics
London School of Economics
and Political Science
University of London

International Economics
Editor: J. Spraos
Professor of Economics
University College London

Labour Economics
Editor: K. J. W. Alexander
Professor of Economics
University of Strathclyde

Macroeconomics
Editor: R. W. Clower
Professor of Economics
University of California
Los Angeles

Microeconomics
Editor: B. J. McCormick
Senior Lecturer in Economics
University of Sheffield

Political Economy
Editor: K. J. W. Alexander
Professor of Economics
University of Strathclyde

G. K. Helleiner

International Trade and Economic Development

Penguin Books

Penguin Books Ltd, Harmondsworth,
Middlesex, England
Penguin Books Inc., 7110 Ambassador Road
Baltimore, Md 21207, USA
Penguin Books Australia Ltd,
Ringwood, Victoria, Australia

First published 1972
Copyright © G. K. Helleiner, 1972

Made and printed in Great Britain by
Cox & Wyman Ltd,
London, Reading and Fakenham
Set in Monotype Times Roman

Penguin Modern Economics Texts

This volume is one in a series of unit texts designed to reduce the price of knowledge for students of economics in universities and colleges of higher education. The units may be used singly or in combination with other units to form attractive and unusual teaching programmes. The volumes will cover the major teaching areas but they will differ from conventional books in their attempt to chart and explore new directions in economic thinking. The traditional divisions of theory and applied, of positive and normative, and of micro and macro will tend to be blurred as authors impose new and arresting ideas on the traditional corpus of economics. Some units will fall into conventional patterns of thought but many will transgress established beliefs.

Penguin Modern Economics Texts are published in units in order to achieve certain objectives. First, a large range of short texts at inexpensive prices gives the teacher flexibility in planning his course and recommending texts for it. Secondly, the pace at which important new work is published requires the project to be adaptable. Our plan allows a unit to be revised or a fresh unit to be added with maximum speed and minimal cost to the reader.

The international range of authorship will, it is hoped, bring out the richness and diversity in economic analysis and thinking.

B. J. McCORMICK

To
Jane, Eric and Peter,
who helped

Contents

Editorial Foreword

Development economics is one of the newer branches of economics and is concerned with the explanation of under-development and with measures to overcome it. Viewed in this light it is essentially a branch of political economy in which political, social and institutional factors cannot be neglected.

There is a case for the view that Adam Smith was the first development economist. But although current interest in the subject has rightly directed attention to neglected 'development aspects' in the writings of a number of eighteenth and nineteenth century economists, their central interests, and those of their successors writing in the early part of the twentieth century lay for the most part elsewhere. Indeed, few of the latter were centrally interested in growth and hardly any in underdevelopment. In the last twenty years there has been a great growth of interest in this area, which has accompanied decolonization and which reflects the growing concern of international society with the poorer, under-developed, three quarters of the globe. In the course of it, development economics has emerged, not without controversy, as a separate area of study.

One of the most important areas of the subject has to do with the role of external economic relationships in the development process. For today's less developed countries, the problems involved in relying on foreign trade to stimulate economic development are many and in crucial respects different from the past. As this book is being published, the third session of the United Nations Conference on Trade and Development is taking place in Chile, providing a world-wide forum in which these problems will be widely debated.

From this Conference the less developed countries will look for the practical implementation of trade policy and othef measures on the part of the advanced countries which may lessen the external constraints upon their development.

In this book the author delineates those characteristics or the international scene which are of particular significance for the development of the poorer countries, and analyses the policy instruments which they themselves may employ to attain their developmental objectives through trade. Professor Helleiner who has much experience of working in developing countries, has written a fresh and skilful analysis of the economic issues in this area. The author brings together recent trends of analytical thinking and the results of a wide range of recent empirical research have been fully taken into account to provide a scrupulously balanced statement. The text is an immensely useful introduction not only to students of economics but to all who are concerned with understanding the issues in this field.

Preface

The writing of a short book in any field involves the selection of particular aspects thereof for emphasis. This survey of the field of international economics with special reference to the trade problems and policies of the less developed countries is no exception. It would be very surprising if many informed readers did not disagree with the emphases I have chosen. It may help, however, if I explain what my ambitions have been. I have tried to write a book which both outlines the major characteristics of the world economic scene as it relates to the external trade of the poor nations, and which explains the policy instruments that can be employed, in poor and rich nations alike, to facilitate the attainment of developmental objectives through international trade. It is thus an attempt to survey both the economics 'of' trade and development, and economics 'for' trade and development.

I have attempted to incorporate the results of recent empirical research wherever possible, so as to avoid an overly theoretical and generalized approach and to keep the content up to date. It is my hope that this book, short as it is, will effectively serve to introduce and summarize an enormously important field of development and international economics for readers both in rich nations and poor, and for non-economists as well as economics students.

I am very grateful to Professor Peter Robson for his helpful comments on the original draft, to Donald Mead and Harry Eastman who made constructive suggestions for its improvement, to Linda Freeman for having assisted in its preparation, and to Mrs Erene Stanley and Miss Irene Kenyon for having patiently typed successive drafts. The responsibility for its remaining shortcomings rests, of course, solely with me.

1 Foreign Trade and Economic Development

Foreign trade has played a strategic role in the historical development of Asia, Africa and Latin America. Production for export typically makes up between 10 and 25 per cent of the total gross domestic product in these areas and still higher proportions of monetary GDP and gross national product. Imports account for an equally large share of aggregate national expenditures. Commodity exports are by far the most important source of foreign exchange earnings in the less developed countries, accounting for over three times the value of gross capital flows into these countries (see Table 1). Foreign trade has also been a major source of government revenue through import and export duties, Marketing Board trading surpluses, multiple exchange rate practices, and company taxes, royalty and rental payments.

These are reasons enough for considerable and separate emphasis to be given to the foreign trade experiences and policies of the developing countries. Exports, imports and economic development are clearly interrelated. These interrelationships are complex and can be expected to vary in their particulars from country to country; but they *are* amenable to economic analysis. Concern with the foreign trade aspects of these countries' development problems in the wealthier countries springs from the fact that it is through trade that their own actions and policies impinge most obviously upon the 'widening gap' between the rich countries and the poor.

History

The nineteenth and early twentieth centuries witnessed an enormous and unprecedented burst in world trade. Part of this phenomenon was an even more rapid rate of growth in production for export in the developing countries of Asia, Africa and Latin America. This latter expansion was almost exclusively in the export of primary produce; and it occurred, by and large, in one of three ways – through mining development, estate or plantation development, and growth in peasant agricultural production for export. In the case of mining and estate develop-

Table 1 **Selected components of the balance of payments of the less developed countries as a whole, 1960–69** (in $US billions)

	1960–62	1965–7	1969
Receipts			
Commodity exports	26·9	37·2	49·8
Official flows (gross)	5·6	7·9	8·3
Private investment	3·3	4·9	5·9
Net services and private transfer payments	0·3	0·4	0·6
Total	36·1	50·4	64·6
Uses			
Commodity imports	30·1	39·5	49·0
Debt service	2·2	3·2	
Other investment payments	3·2	4·9	14·2
Miscellaneous	1·0	1·5	
Changes in reserves	−0·4	+1·3	+1·4
Total	36·1	50·4	64·6

Sources: UNCTAD (1969).
UN *Monthly Bulletin of Statistics.*
OECD (1970), *Development Assistance Review.*
IMF, *International Financial Statistics.*

ment, substantial inputs of foreign capital and manpower were involved directly in the production process; in that of peasant agriculture these inputs from abroad were of less significance and tended to be concentrated in the commercial sector rather than in production itself.

In all cases, of course, the expansion in exports was part of the broader pattern of European imperial expansion into these parts of the world, which had not previously been so directly or so massively involved in the European economic system. The economic gains from this expansion probably accrued both to the European powers and to the colonies and satellites (although as will be seen, the latter point is in some dispute), but no one would argue that they were, in any sense, 'equitably' distributed as between the metropolitan centres and their representatives in the periphery, on the one hand, and the periphery itself, on the other. The power of the European metropole to coerce and to control, the concentration of economic power and market strength within many of the European industries engaging in overseas investment and trade, and the relatively weak market strength of the inhabitants of the host economies, combined to turn the terms of whatever bargains were struck to the advantage of the metropolitan interests, even if those in the host countries may still have been 'better off' than if the bargains had not been struck at all. Orthodox economists attribute the unequal outcome to relative market strengths coupled with a degree of colonial coercion. Marxists see it as a logical consequence of the exploitative capitalist system, which brought with it further large surpluses that played an important role in the historical development of the metropolitan countries themselves.

There is a considerable history of controversy over the interrelationship between international trade and economic development over the course of the last century or so in the less developed areas. On the one hand are those who emphasize the positive effects of international exchange and capital flows upon the growth of poor countries. Their case rests principally upon the conventional static argument of comparative advantage theory – that countries should produce that which they are relatively most suited for (or those commodities which are intensive in the use of those factors with which they are relatively well endowed). From this it follows that the introduction of international trade permitted increased specialization and increased international trade in the nations in question, which together must have led the inhabitants to a higher level of income than that with which they began. An important variant of this argument hypothesizes that the opening of world markets to the produce of these areas created a 'vent' for the surplus (or potential surplus) production of the area in question, which did not in fact reallocate its employed resources but, rather, through participation in the world market economy, increased its use of available resources formerly underemployed. The other main thrust of the argument emphasizing the beneficial effects of trade in the historical context is the 'classical' one which focuses upon the role of trade as an 'engine of growth' generating a variety of dynamic 'educative' effects – increased knowledge of production and organizational techniques, altered demand patterns, and other learning effects from specialization, all of which increase productivity and alter the production function itself.

On the other hand, many authors have pointed out the possible detrimental impact upon development of participation in the world economy and have argued that, historically, the effect of such participation in the less developed areas has, on balance, been negative. These authors have emphasized the enclave character of much of the export development and the 'backwash' effects it has thrown off for the rest of the economy, the export bias which has been imparted to the infrastructure of the economy, the social and economic stratification which has accompanied it, the destruction of indigenous industries by imported substitutes, the demonstration effects which have tended to lower savings propensities and impede domestic capital formation, the over-rapid use of exhaustible resources and the tendency for the commodity terms of trade to deteriorate secularly. The argument has been a long and vehement one to which the only safe conclusion must be that the historical impact of exports has varied considerably from place to place and that there have been negative as well as positive effects from export development in the developing countries.

Orthodox comparative cost theory would interpret the 'opening up' of the Third World to world markets in terms of a shift along the production possibilities frontier in Figure 1 from A to B, a shift towards increased production of exportables. The 'vent for surplus' explanation runs in terms of a shift from a point inside the frontier, like X, to the frontier itself, say at B; the utilization of formerly un- or underemployed resources and/or labour enables production of exportables to expand without any sacrifice in the production of other goods and services. Those who have been concerned with

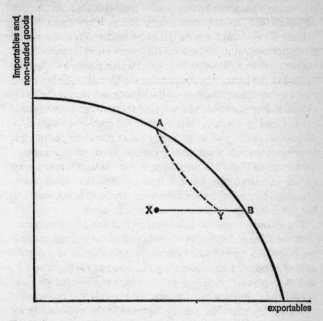

Figure 1

the effects upon indigenous industries and the disruptive effects of shifting the production structure would portray the shift from *A* to *B* as taking place not along the production possibilities frontier but along a path inside (perhaps well inside) it, such as that shown by the dotted arc *A Y*; if the adjustment is particularly difficult the economy might be considered never actually to have arrived at *B* and to remain inside the production frontier, say at *Y*. The dynamic learning effects would be shown by an outward shift in the whole production possibilities frontier.

The terms of trade

The detailed pros and cons of these arguments have been rehearsed in a number of other readily available sources, and will not, therefore, be elaborated here. The primary focus of this volume is upon the formulation of present and future external trade policies rather than upon historical interpretation.

On one matter, however, it may be worth saying a little more in view of the light it sheds upon the analysis of trade flows and terms today. This is the issue of the historical trends in the terms of trade. For purposes of analysing the average international prices faced by a particular country in the course of its development or over any particular historical or planning period, it is important to distinguish among various alternative concepts of the 'terms of trade'. In particular, it is most useful to consider the commodity (or net barter) terms of trade, the income terms of trade, and the single factoral terms of trade. (There are others, but for our purposes these three are sufficient.)

The controversy over historical trends has been concerned with the commodity terms of trade – the relationship between the price of a typical unit of exports and the price of a typical unit of imports. This is normally expressed as P_x/P_m, where P_x and P_m represent price indices, with base periods the same, of exports and imports respectively. (In the UK the commodity terms of trade are frequently inverted.) The procedures for appropriately weighting the components of the export and import bills need not concern us here.

Both for historical interpretation and for planning purposes, it may be more important to know the change in the volume of imports which can be purchased with a given volume of factor inputs in the export sector, rather than that in the imports purchasable with a given volume of exports. For this purpose, the relevant concept is the 'single factoral terms of trade', which allows for changes in factor productivity in the export sector. This is defined as $E_x.P_x/P_m$, where E_x is an index of productivity in the export sector based in the same year as the export and import price indices. Productivity indices are notoriously difficult to estimate, but the objective sought through the use

Index of adaptability to buy imports (Total)

of this concept is clear enough – it is to estimate the real factor income changes in the export sector in terms of purchasing power for imports.

The 'income terms of trade' measures alterations in the import purchasing power of exports, making allowance for changes in export volume. For planning a foreign exchange budget this concept may well be the most useful. It is defined as $Q_x.P_x/P_m$, where Q_x is an index of export volume with the same base year as the two price indices. Expressed differently, it is an index of total export receipts (price times volume) deflated by an import price index. It is cogently argued that deflation of export value, to eliminate the effects of price changes in the estimation of real GNP or GDP for export-dependent economies, should be handled differently from price deflation of other components thereof; the idea is to replace an export volume measure (constant-price exports where the deflator is an export price index) with a measure of the income terms of trade (constant-price exports where the deflator is an import price index).

All three concepts normally exclude non-merchandise trade (although all transport services are implicitly included as imports because of the convention of measuring imports at c.i.f. prices and exports at f.o.b. prices). Thus no account is taken of the effects of price alterations upon the real value of capital inflows or foreign exchange reserves. It is quite possible for the commodity terms of trade to remain unaltered through proportional increases in the prices of exports and imports, yet for the country in question to be made considerably worse off because of the reduced purchasing power of its foreign capital inflow and foreign exchange reserves.

The discussion of secular trends in the commodity terms of trade, based originally upon the observation that the British terms of trade had improved markedly between the 1870s and the late 1930s, and buttressed by some theoretical explanations of the 'necessity' for continued deterioration of the terms of trade of primary-producing poor countries, has demonstrated, above all else, the difficulty of making historical generalizations with imperfect data. Effective attacks have been made both upon the data and the theoretical analysis underlying the 'Prebisch thesis'. One is therefore forced to remain fairly agnostic about historical trends in the commodity terms of trade.

Whatever one might conclude about the statistical evidence it would not, in any case, prove anything about the prospects for the future course of the terms of trade. There is no substitute for careful forecasting, country by country and commodity by commodity. Even so, policies pursued in consequence of forecasts as to international price prospects may well have the effect of negating the original forecasts; where, as unfortunately is normally the case in poor countries, the forecasts are not too optimistic, their negation is one of the principal objects of foreign trade strategy. Thus, neither failure of the statistical evidence to support the thesis of secularly deteriorating commodity terms of trade nor failure of a forecast deterioration in these terms to materialize constitute grounds for rejection of the notion that poor primary-producing countries usually face very great market difficulties and price prospects (see chapter 2). No doubt this sort of conclusion – to the effect that 'it all depends' – is not very satisfying to those seeking simple interpretations of the world international economic scene; but the scene is not a simple one.

It should be obvious by now that deterioration in the commodity terms of trade, which has received so much emphasis in the literature of development economics, need not be accompanied either by declining export receipts, if volume expands sufficiently, nor by declining income in the export sector, if export productivity expands sufficiently; and it certainly need not carry declining national income with it since there are other sectors in the economy. What one *can* say is that deterioration in the commodity terms of trade leaves the country in question with lower foreign exchange earnings and lower national income than if the deterioration had not occurred; but such a deterioration may be implicit in a strategy of export expansion which is geared to national income objectives, in which case it is merely a reflection of the bad market prospects for some of the export commodities. It is these market problems which are at the core of the international trading problem, then, and not the 'necessary' trends in the commodity or any other terms of trade. Obviously, which concept of the terms of trade one focuses on depends upon what it is that one wants to know.

Table 2 shows the commodity and income terms of trade, using 1963 as the base year, for the developing countries in 1969. Clearly, one forms a rather more optimistic picture from the income terms of trade than one does from the commodity terms of trade, although even the latter have not actually been deteriorating in most areas in recent years. (It is not difficult to show deterioration through the use of an alternative base year.) Export volume increases have made it possible for poor countries to finance expanding volumes of imports despite the absence of any strongly favourable trends in their commodity terms of trade.

Table 2 Income and commodity terms of trade, 1969 (1963 = 100)

	terms of trade Commodity	terms of trade Income
Africa	108	174
Latin America	103	130
Middle East	94	164
Other Asia	103	151
Total developing countries	102	151

Source: UN, *Monthly Bulletin of Statistics.*

Despite the obvious importance of import prices to the foreign trade of the less developed countries, an importance made explicit in all three of the above-mentioned concepts of the terms of trade, the discussion in the remainder of this volume will be devoted almost exclusively to export prospects and problems. While improved policies with respect to import purchasing might significantly improve individual nations' overall performance on international account, their room for manoeuvre is in most cases very small and world prices for imports have, therefore, to be taken as more or less 'given'.

The character of the export sector

Of greater interest than the global arguments to prove or disprove the thesis that exports have assisted in the development process is a consideration of the factors which influenced the domestic impact in each particular historical situation. What has been the legacy of the export sector for the development planner today? It is on this front that some of the more interesting research and writing has been conducted, and it is from this approach that we may derive some conclusions as to the probable longer-term impact of development along different export expansion paths in the future.

One fundamental element in estimating the impact of an export sector's development upon the development of the entire economy in which it is located is the extent to which the incomes earned therein accrue to the nationals of the host country. Who owns the land, the capital, and the skill? And of what nationality is the labour? In an archetype enclave, foreigners pay minimal rent for the right to use the land, use their own foreign capital, hire employees from abroad, and leave minimal impact upon the rest of the country even though they may create significant export development. It is therefore crucial to distinguish between gross *domestic* product which is a measure of the value of output within the geographic boundaries of the political unit in question, and gross *national* product which measures the income earned by the host-country nationals within that unit. Where there is substantial foreign participation in the export (or, for that matter, any other) sector, the gross domestic product will be much larger than the gross national product; and the growth in one may not be correlated with the growth in the other. It is even possible for the value of exports to exceed the gross national product! A useful tool, employed in a study of the export sector in Chile, is the concept of 'returned value' which not only measures, for each year, the earnings accruing to the nation directly from within the export sector (principally wages and taxes), but also adds in the value of domestic purchases whether for intermediate inputs or investment purposes (Reynolds, 1963). The national share of the income accruing from the export sector is obviously the most important single factor in assessing the total developmental impact.

The characteristics of the income distribution within the host nation are also an important element in assessing the legacy of the traditional export sector. In large part this is the product of the production function. Where, as in the case of most mining sectors, production is fairly capital-intensive, the bulk of the national share is likely to take the form of taxes upon (foreign) profits which will presumably be used primarily to support government employees. Those wage-earners fortunate enough to obtain employment in the capital-intensive industry are likely to be remunerated well relatively to the rest of the economy, and their wages will govern the rate at which state employees are paid. Employment in the government and mining sectors will be concentrated geographically as well. There will therefore be a tendency for the distribution of income and access to services to be highly skewed and, where there is exogenously determined rural–urban migration, for severe unemployment problems to manifest themselves. This concentration of income may also affect the pattern of national demand and thus the import bill and the nature of early-stage industrialization, pushing them all in the direction of more luxury-goods; it may also influence the educational system and/or engender deepseated negative attitudes towards business pursuits and manual labour.

At the other extreme is the pattern of development from a peasant export base. In this case, incomes are likely to be much more widely spread, the social infrastructure to be geographically dispersed, and the pattern of demand to be oriented towards necessities of life and rural production requisites. It could be argued that in the latter case, savings propensities are also likely to be lower in the aggregate.

As was suggested above, the production characteristics of the export sector are of considerable importance for the aggregate developmental impact. This is not merely a matter of their effect upon the distribution of national income, important as that is. More fundamentally, the factor-intensity of the export sector, which has been found to vary greatly, in large part determines the national share of the product itself. If the export production process is capital- and/or skill-intensive when the economy in question has an endowment heavily weighted in favour of unskilled labour, the scarce factors will inevitably have to be imported in the short-run and, perhaps, even in the longer-run as well, with the result that a considerable share of the increased total value of export production will have to be devoted to the remuneration of foreign factors of production. (Contrary to the assumptions of orthodox international trade theory, certain factors of production – notably capital and skill – are highly mobile internationally. They are, moreover, frequently relatively immobile within developing countries.) Foreign factor imports create a 'larger pie' of which the national share is small. Failure of the production technology to 'fit' the factor endowment may, at the same time, produce greater learning effects which alter some of the endowments since it is usually economic for firms to train locals in the necessary skills for the production process.

Linkage effects also vary with different types of export production. The possibilities for processing primary products of different sorts are dependent upon the factor-intensities and the potential for scale economies in the processing activities, the structure of transport rates, and the location of markets for the final products. The possibilities for domestic sources of supply of various production inputs and capital equipment depend upon a similar matrix of influences. These linkage prospects are likely in any case to be dwarfed by the importance of 'final demand linkages' arising out of the pattern of demand of the national income recipients in the export sector and eventually, as development proceeds, of all income earners throughout the economy.

The infrastructural requirements also differ with different patterns of export growth. The transport facilities required by a peasant agricultural exporting economy are totally different from those demanded by an economy the export progress of which is determined by a mine or two or by petroleum deposits. A widespread network of feeder roads is likely to be found in the case of the former whereas a railway line from mines to port may be sufficient in the latter. The social overhead demanded by a primarily foreign labour force – in the form of paved roads, schools, hospitals, etc., at least within the area of their employment – will also be much more concentrated and more skill- and capital-intensive than in the case where the labour force is primarily indigenous as with a peasant export sector. This infrastructure may itself throw off linkage effects and/or learning effects which differ, depending upon its character. All of these effects, like the linkage effects discussed above, will of course be reduced in importance as overall growth proceeds.

In that independent governments are now able to some degree to manage the export sectors in the national interest if they so choose, the importance of these 'natural' tendencies to develop in particular and divergent patterns as a result of beginning with different export commodities is today somewhat diminished. While this sort of 'staple theory' of development is therefore primarily of historical interest, it is nevertheless useful in considering the broader implications of reliance upon different types of export development strategies in the future, and analysing the leverage which may be obtained from them in seeking the national goals. In some cases, for instance that of the petroleum-dependent economies, the nature of the staple may be as valid a basis for building generalizable development models as other more conventional ones such as relative factor endowments.

Policy implications

Whatever has been the role of external economic relationships in the development process in the past, the policy question remains. What are the prospects for using foreign trade in the interest of the development effort today? Even if one were to conclude that, all things considered, external trade had had a detrimental effect upon economic growth because of the export bias it had imparted to the economy, deteriorating terms of trade, and so forth, and even if one were pessimistic as to the future prospects in these respects, there is still the policy question of how to formulate trade and investment policies for that future.

At the broadest possible level there is the choice as to whether to use the opportunity for international economic relationships at all. It would be possible for some nations, particularly the larger ones, to opt out of the international economy, if not completely, at least in large part. It is asserted by some analysts that continued reliance upon world markets, the prospects for which are bleak or uncertain, is prejudicial to the development of the fundamental restructuring of the economies of poor nations which alone will produce long-term growth and development. External economic ties are believed by others to be fundamentally exploitative in nature and to generate further 'underdevelopment' rather than development. 'Outward-oriented development is not development but development of under-development' in that the trading and investment relationships implied thereby accentuate the 'structural characteristics of under-development (dislocation and sectoral disparities in productivity)' (Amin, 1971). Only autonomous, self-financed, and self-initiated development in this view can be truly described as development or, indeed, will generate any meaningful change. While this brand of analysis may constitute a healthy rectification of historical imbalance in the traditional views of development strategies for developing countries, it hardly constitutes a prescription for policy except, perhaps, and even this is questionable, in the very long run. If a nation seeks to break out of the overdependence on a few commodity exports, a few external markets, and foreign sources of expertise and capital, which together are frequently characterized as 'neo-colonialist', it still must develop policies to employ to best advantage whatever it at present has in order to attain its own objectives with maximum efficiency.

'The critique of "growth through primary product exports" and of "salvation through foreign capital" should not . . . be viewed as a justification for autarchy, for a lack of attention to export expansion along whatever lines are feasible and viable in a medium-term perspective, or for indifference to securing foreign finance and high-level personnel when these are available on reasonably favourable terms and with a manageable number of strings. Small economies have a very real potential for securing gains from a rational and dynamically changing specialization in production linked to their international as well as regional trade patterns. It is precisely when export growth is low and structural change requires significant increases in imports of capital and industrial input goods that policies to augment and allocate foreign exchange receipts on both current and capital account are most crucial' (Green, 1971, p. 286).

Risk aversion in the face of unstable world markets may constitute a valid basis for an autarchic economic strategy. A preference for autarchy may also spring from a strategy of rapid structural change from primary to (often initially inefficient) industrial production, nationalistic reluctance to become involved in relationships with foreign countries or ideas, or ideological preference for 'self-reliance' as an end in itself. Some writers interpret all economic relationships between poor nations and the rich nations of the West as involving 'dependence' of the former upon the latter, a condition which they also consider to be undesirable of itself. 'Dependence' is therefore to be reduced, in their view, by decreasing the foreign sector's role in aggregate economic activity or, sometimes, by expanding economic relationships with other poor nations or socialist states. Whatever the ultimate motivations for promoting a more autarchic development, such a strategy calls for the meeting of one's own demands from domestic sources of supply wherever possible and, presumably, in considerable disregard of cost, using foreign trade only to acquire goods and services absolutely unavailable at home, to dispose of surpluses, or to make up short-term gaps which were not planned for.

At the other extreme is the strategy of retaining maximum 'openness' in a developing country which is based upon the historical case for free trade, developed in the UK early in its own industrialization process and very much in its own interest. While the basic argument for obtaining gains from trade wherever possible still holds, the classical prescription for completely free trade must be adapted to the present context of the less developed countries. Among the reasons for requiring a more sophisticated application of the tenets of comparative advantage theory than is usually suggested by the fundamentalist 'free trader' are the following: the demand for rapid augmentation of stocks of skill and capital in the poor countries, substantial blockages to free trade throughout the international market system, the presence of monopolistic and oligopolistic elements in world markets, rapid shifts in the composition of demand both internally and in world markets, a distorted infrastructure in the poor nations which supports external trading activities disproportionately, substantial foreign ownership of domestic factors of production in the poor countries and limited price and income elasticities of demand for their present bundle of export goods.

Reliance upon traditional primary product exports, the orthodox colonial strategy for development, has nevertheless produced rapid rates of GNP growth in a fairly large number of poor countries during the past two decades (Chenery, 1971, p. 43). Moreover, a number of empirical studies of developing countries have found significant correlations, both cross-sectionally between countries and within single countries over time, between growth of national income and export growth, although the direction of causation is not always clear (Maizels, 1968, pp. 44–9; Kravis, 1970, p. 160; Chenery, 1971, p. 43). These results have led many scholars to associate successful growth performance with policies of 'openness' and export promotion, although some of these grant that significant shifts may be required in the structures both of production and of trade if growth is to be sustained.

The observed relative size of the export or import sector is largely related to the size of the country. Large countries like India, China, and Brazil have smaller export shares in their total productive activities than the small tropical African or Central American states. On average, the ratio of exports to GDP rises with increases in per capita GNP, but the share of primary products in the rising export share falls with these income increases (Chenery, 1971, p. 31; Kuznets, 1964, 1967). A country may choose a higher or lower degree of openness or autarchy than is usual for its size and level of income. Some have attempted to classify countries according to whether they are 'outward'- or 'inward-looking' in their development strategy. Table 3 shows the import to GDP ratios for a sample of less developed countries over time, and illustrates both the inter-country variance and the variation within single countries over time as their commercial policies and the fortunes of their exports alter.

Table 3 **Imports/GDP in selected underdeveloped countries, 1950–1969**

	1950–52	1957–9	1964–6	1967–9
Argentina	9	11	7	8 (1969)
Brazil	12	10	8	8 (1968)
Mexico	12	11	8	10 (1968)
India	8	7	7	7 (1967)
Pakistan	8	7	10	9 (1968)
Philippines	14	13	19	17 (1969)
Taiwan	13	14	19	27 (1969)
Nigeria	16	19 (1957)	16·5 (1966)	19 (1967)
United Arab Republic	20 (1950)	18 (1959–60)	22 (1966)	17 (1969)

Sources: Little, Scitovsky and Scott (1970, p. 11).
Helleiner (1966).
Mead (1966).
Nigerian Institute of Social and Economic Research (1969).
IMF, *International Financial Statistics*.

Once a country has decided upon the general level of external involvement – and *all* countries pursue external strategies which lie somewhere between the extremes of total autarchy and complete free trade – it must seek to do the best it can with it. The basic theory of comparative advantage correctly states that in conditions of complete information and certainty, every country will maximize its economic welfare by specializing in those activities in which it is relatively most efficient, trading the products of other activities in which it is relatively inefficient. The open questions are those of which time period one is working within, how variable one's relative efficiencies in various activities are over time, how to treat the problem of uncertainty, and whether one has other 'non-economic' objectives.

In order to make the most out of external trade, one must obviously seek to dynamize the static comparative advantage analysis to permit the analysis of likely and feasible fields for international specialization and trade some decades hence, allowing for altered factor endowments, external economies, diseconomies and market imperfections, the prospect of alterations in the structure of trade barriers, and the inter-relationships between factor accumulation and the structure of production during the interim. The prediction of future fields for efficient specialization is certainly not an easy matter. One ought at least, however, to be able to project the directions of appropriate longer-run change and to be considerably more specific for medium-term objectives. If one can, then, as part of the general development strategy, ascertain the structure of import and export trade which is to be the target, one can mobilize the various policy instruments which can be employed to achieve it, among which the commercial and exchange rate policies discussed below in chapters 7–9 are prominent.

The underdeveloped countries do have some room for manoeuvre and some options for policy in their economic relationships with the rest of the world. In order to make the most of them, they must understand the constraints of the international economic scene and the basic tools of analysis and policy which are available for their use within these constraints. To these we now turn.

2 Commodity Problems

While considerable success has been realized by some less developed countries in the export of processed and semi-processed products in the 1960s, the great bulk of the Third World's export earnings are still from primary products (see Table 4). Total world primary product exports have grown more slowly in recent years than world trade, and the developing countries' share of these exports has been falling. The literature of economics has devoted considerable space to discussion of 'commodity problems' – unsatisfactory trends in their prices, and problems with price instability – but there are early limits to the usefulness of generalizations about primary product exports. Useful discussions arrive fairly quickly at the level of individual commodities and countries. One can begin to sense this by considering the variety of products of major importance in Third World sales shown in Table 5 and the divergent price trends for commodity groups shown in Table 6. The commodity problems of a Middle-Eastern petroleum-producing country are very different from those of an Asian tea-producing country, which are different again from those of an African cotton exporter. Since this is a short and general book, however, compromises must be made. The discussion in this chapter will be concerned with the question of international market prospects for the two major commodity categories (agricultural and non-agricultural). In the next chapter the possibilities for *international* action to improve the prices and earnings of Third World commodity producers will be explored.

Table 4 **Composition of total exports from less developed countries, 1953/5–1969** ($ US billions)

	1953–5	1958–60	1963–5	1969
Food, beverages and tobacco	8·8	9·2	11·3	11·8
Raw materials (excluding fuels)	6·4	7·0	8·3	9·7[1]
Agricultural	4·3	4·5	4·7	n.a.
Non-agricultural (minerals and metals)	2·2	2·5	3·6	n.a.
Mineral fuels and related materials	5·3	7·5	10·5	16·3
Manufactured products	1·7	2·2	3·9	12·0[1]
Total	22·3	26·0	34·1	49·8

1. 1969 data for raw materials and manufactures are not comparable with the data for earlier years since non-ferrous metals (SITC 68) are included in 'manufactured products' in 1969, but more appropriately, in non-agricultural 'raw materials' in earlier years.

Sources: International Bank for Reconstruction and Development (1969).
UN, *Monthly Bulletin of Statistics*

Demand factors
Agricultural products

As far as most agricultural exports from developing countries are concerned, the demand prospects are constrained by the following complex of factors.

1. The (per capita) income elasticities of demand for agricultural raw materials, foodstuffs and tropical beverages are low in the richer countries which constitute the poor countries' principal markets. (Some of the available estimates are shown in Table 7.) In part, this phenomenon is the product of the changing industrial structure which accompanies economic growth, the shift to service industries and less material-using manufacturing activities. For other commodities, demand seems to be already at or near the saturation point, e.g. coffee in the US market, tea in the UK. Total demand prospects are, in any case, not the same as prospects for imports; in some

instances, notably in the cases of temperate agricultural products, oilseeds, and sugar, production trends in the importing countries must also be considered.

Only the *remarkable* and sustained rates of growth of the industrial nations were able to maintain the modest rates of growth of agricultural exports from poor nations in the 1960s. The demand implications of rising levels of income are potentially impressive only in the socialist states of Eastern Europe, where demand for tropical products has been restrained by the planners well below the levels 'normal' for unplanned economies of equivalent incomes, and in other poor countries which may themselves be producers or potential producers of the commodities in question.

2. Population growth rates in the present principal markets for these products are also modest (0·7 per cent to 1·4 per cent, averaging about 1·1 per cent in total, Maizels, 1968, p. 110), so that little expansion in demand can be expected from this source either.

3. The price-elasticity of world demand for most tropical agricultural commodities appears to be low, although the empirical evidence on this point is far from conclusive, since it is taken from a limited range of observations over a series of short cycles. (Table 7 presents some rough price-elasticity estimates.) The low demand elasticity at the retail level for final products using tropical agricultural inputs, e.g. soaps, chocolates, roasted coffee, together with the low share of the raw material in the value of the final product – when account is taken of processing and packaging costs, transport, markups, and taxes – and the frequent high degree of market concentration at the processing level, all create strong grounds for expecting the price-elasticity of demand at the level of the raw material market to be very low.

The price-elasticity of demand facing any one producing country may, of course, be high if its share of the world market is sufficiently small. In general, the price-elasticity of demand facing one producing country is the reciprocal of the world-market share times the world elasticity, plus a factor reflecting the supply elasticity of other producers.

Table 5 Exports of commodities of principal interest to developing countries, 1963-5

	Exports from developing countries, 1963-5 average[1] (1)	World exports, 1963-5 average[1] (2)	Share of developing countries in world exports (1) as a per cent of (2) (3)	Share of commodity in total exports from developing countries, 1963-5 average (4)	Number of developing countries for which exports of commodity exceed 5% of total exports (5)
	Million US dollars				
Petroleum	9730	11,990	81·1	28·9	18
Coffee	2190	2190	100·0	6·5	26
Sugar	1565	1995	78·5	4·6	19
Cotton	1285	2010	63·9	3·8	22
Rubber	1175	1210	97·2	3·5	9
Copper	1150	1390	82·8	3·4	7
Timber	785	4370	17·9	2·3	15
Iron ore	630	1335	47·0	1·9	11
Tea	590	640	92·2	1·8	6
Rice	585	835	69·9	1·7	8
Cocoa	510	515	98·8	1·5	7
Jute textiles	440	530	83·0	1·3	2
Tin	375	380	99·5	1·1	7
Bananas	340	360	93·9	1·0	10
Cotton textiles	320	1230	26·2	1·0	4

Beef	320	0·9	980	32·7	6
Tobacco	320	0·9	1030	31·0	4
Wheat	295	0·9	2895	10·2	1
Maize	285	0·8	1155	24·5	4
Copra	270	0·8	270	100·0	3
Wool	255	0·8	1840	13·8	2
Groundnuts	230	0·7	255	89·8	7
Bauxite	210	0·6	225	92·5	4
Phosphate rock	190	0·6	250	75·0	4
Hides and skins	165	0·5	425	39·2	3
Jute	175	0·5	175	100·0	2
Fishmeal	160	0·5	255	62·2	1
Sisal	150	0·4	160	94·9	6
Zinc	120	0·4	270	44·6	1
Manganese	115	0·3	135	83·2	1
Palm oil	115	0·3	120	95·8	3
Coconut oil	115	0·3	130	89·2	3
Lead	110	0·3	240	46·6	1
Groundnut oil	105	0·3	125	81·9	2

1. Rounded to the nearest US $5 million; the percentage figures in subsequent columns are based on the unrounded data.
Source: International Monetary Fund–International Bank for Reconstruction and Development (1969).

Table 6 Index of selected commodity prices, 1960–70
(1960–62 = 100)

	Total index (including petroleum)	Total index (excluding petroleum)	Food	Agricultural non-food	Metals and ores	Others[1]
1960	104	104	104	108	102	97
1961	99	99	98	98	100	100
1962	97	97	98	94	98	102
1963	101	104	116	93	98	99
1964	104	110	119	94	127	98
1965	103	111	107	94	151	106
1966	104	113	109	92	163	106
1967	100	107	111	86	133	106
1968	101	108	111	88	138	110
1969	107	118	121	95	156	115
1970 1st quarter	111	124	128	96	172	116

1. Timber, textiles and fishmeal.
Source: World Bank, International Development Association (1970), *Annual Report*, p. 45.

4. Rapid technological change is producing cheap and often qualitatively superior synthetic substitutes for many agricultural products, e.g. rubber, wool and cotton, sisal and jute, hides and skins, etc. The market share of natural products in these cases is falling steadily (see Table 8). This has the side effect of raising world price-elasticity of demand at or near the level of synthetic prices.

Research and development efforts are also producing means of lowering the raw material inputs per unit of those final products which employ natural inputs, through improved stock control, reduced losses in transport and handling, and the development of blends of materials and synthetics. To some extent, such technological advances constitute once-for-all demand reductions, but their institutionalization in the modern corporation makes further such developments fairly predictable. Research expenditures on the development of synthetic substitutes for tropical agricultural produce were recently

Table 7 Estimated income- and price-elasticities of demand for selected agricultural products in industrial country markets

	Income	Price (negative)
Coffee	0·8	under 0·5
Natural rubber	n.a.	0·5–1·0
Sugar	0·4	under 0·5
Cocoa	0·5	under 0·5
Lauric acid, oils and oilseeds	0·4–0·7	0·5–1·0
Hard fibres	0·7	under 0·5
Tea	0·1	0·5–1·0
Bananas	0·2–0·7	0·5–1·0

Sources: Maizels (1968, p. 110).
Proceedings of the United Nations Conference on Trade and Development (1968, p. 26).
Rojko and Mackie (1970, pp. 8–9).

estimated at $1 billion annually! (IMF–IBRD, 1968, p. 110).

Research into the development of further end uses for primary products such as was successfully undertaken with respect to jute products, obviously has a beneficial counter-effect in that it may shift the demand curve and increase income-elasticity of demand; but this has so far been of relatively small importance.

5. Agricultural protection in the richer countries limits market access, sometimes physically, for poor countries' agricultural exports, and this protection is not on the wane. The new common agricultural policies of the European Economic Community, for instance, are *more* restrictive of imports on many products imported from developing countries than those in existence before. It is not merely the *fact* of protection which is harmful but, more specifically, its *form*. The replacement of quotas and tariffs by direct subsidies would substantially reduce the dimensions of the problem (see chapter 3). Not only, then, does there exist a constant market barrier to certain agricultural exports which must be overcome, but there may even be *increasing* barriers over time as exporters respond to increasing

Table 8 **Shares of natural products in total consumption in industrial countries, mid-1950s to 1975**

	Mid-1950s	Mid-1960s	1975 projected
Natural rubber's share of total rubber consumption	62	36	28
Cotton's share of total apparel fibre consumption	41	34	29

Source: Maizels (1968, pp, 333, 358).
Proceedings of the United Nations Conference on Trade and Development (1968, p. 349).

competitive power in other countries. This is primarily a problem, of course, for those products which are also produced in the richer countries, such as temperate foodstuffs, oil seeds and sugar. Unfortunately, the prospect of finding markets in other poor countries may also be constrained by protectionist policies; agricultural self-sufficiency is a frequent high-priority policy objective there as well.

The prospects for some 'agricultural' products are rather brighter than these generalities would suggest. In particular, timber and timber products, and fish and fish products are instances in which income-elasticities are favourable and overall demand prospects for poor exporting countries fairly bright. If protection can be overcome the same could be said for meat and meat products.

Minerals, metals and fuels

The value of developing-country exports of minerals, base metals and fuels has risen far more rapidly than that of agricultural commodities and is expected, all things considered, to continue to rise fairly rapidly. UNCTAD projections see them accounting for half of total developing-country exports by the mid-1970s. Unfortunately, petroleum and mineral exports are highly concentrated in a relatively few poor countries; one estimate places 90 per cent of total exports of this type from the developing countries in countries making up only one-fourth of the Third World's total population (Mikesell *et al.*, 1971, pp. 3–6).

The demand prospects for most metals and mineral ores – the main ones are iron ore, manganese, copper, bauxite, tin, lead and zinc – not to speak of petroleum, are generally much better than for agricultural products. The income-elasticity of demand is believed to be relatively high. Non-ferrous metal consumption, for example, is highly correlated with manufacturing production in the major industrial countries; and the 'output elasticity of demand' (for consumption, not import) for non-ferrous metals in the industrial countries is, on average, close to unity (Maizels, 1968, p. 387). While protection exists, it is more frequently absent, and import demand can be expected to rise at a rate at least as rapid as that of consumption. Moreover, technological advance has probably, on balance, augmented total world demand for minerals, while no doubt altering its composition, especially towards petroleum and bauxite. Some economies on mineral inputs have, however, been achieved through new processing techniques such as electrolytic tinplating.

While static price elasticity of demand is usually low, except where there is substitutability with wood, plastics or other inputs, this is not such a serious constraint when other factors are favourable; supplies are, in any case, more susceptible to controls than is usual in the case of agricultural products.

The demand problems for mineral producers relate more to assuring themselves, as individual countries, of reasonable shares of the expanding world market and fair shares of the resulting profits, in negotiations with international producing firms, than to working out strategies for coping with world markets themselves; for there is typically a high degree of foreign ownership and market concentration in the world petroleum and mineral trade (Mikesell *et al.*, 1971, p. 9). Even where, in recent years, there have been dramatic changes in the direction of local ownership, concentration in marketing and production expertise remains.

Where domestic production is concentrated in the hands of one or a handful of foreign firms which also control international processing and marketing and have production activities located in a variety of other countries, the object of the host countries' government must be to pay no more for the required inputs of capital, skill and marketing services than the going international price, and thereby to keep for the host country the rent which accrues to the scarce resource. The most striking cases of this type are the petroleum, copper and bauxite (aluminium) operations in the Middle East, Africa and Latin America. Timber and bananas are non-mineral examples of similar cases. Historically, of course, the foreign firms have been accustomed to receiving a substantial portion of these resource rents themselves. Conflict between the foreign firms and the host governments are inevitable; in the absence of competitive markets for the goods and services in question, the outcomes are indeterminate within quite a wide range.

Greatly increased sophistication on the part of host countries – together with increased co-operation among them – has made it possible to improve the prices and earnings from primary products considerably in recent years through more effective bargaining with foreign firms. This bargaining may be concerned with the tax rate, royalty and rental payments, the prices at which the produced materials are sold to affiliates in other countries, wage rates for local labour, the development of local processing, the use of local inputs and the prices of foreign ones. At times these negotiations have also been concerned with the rate of local exploitation, i.e. supply policy. Local participation in management decisions on an ongoing basis, instead of through periodic negotiations on an arms-length basis between host government and foreign firms, and an increased degree of local ownership are also sometimes part of the bargain. These may seem to be matters for the analysis of direct foreign investment but they are, in many instances, inseparable from the commodity question.

Supply factors

What eventually becomes of commodity prices and incomes will obviously depend on supply as well as demand factors. There is, in principle, an optimizing supply policy for each individual country and also one for the relevant producing countries as a group, though the uncertainties on both the demand and supply side complicate the issue. It would clearly be a mistake, for instance, to expand production and export of a commodity in a range in which the price-elasticity was less than unity. Similarly, restrictive supply policies, whether conscious or not, should not be pursued, other things being equal, when the world market can readily absorb greater quantities.

World demand conditions, with some possible modifications through advertising and new product-use research, must be accepted as more or less given. An understanding of world demand conditions must, of course, incorporate a detailed knowledge of the various special arrangements, bulk purchase contracts, commodity agreements, preferential duties and market sharing agreements which surround the world markets for commodities such as sugar, bananas and petroleum. Armed with the relevant information about world demand characteristics and prospects, it should be possible to construct both short- and longer-run supply strategies in order to take best advantage of the world market prospects. There are obviously other elements also in the formulation of export supply strategy in individual countries besides the world market forecasts. As will be seen in chapter 3, there are also likely to be joint gains from co-ordinating supply policies with other relevant exporting nations. Instruments of commercial, tax and exchange rate policy can then be mobilized in pursuit of the agreed objectives.

It is not always possible, of course, either to expand or to contract supplies flexibly in response to policy-makers' perceptions of market prospects. One of the primary characteristics of under-developed countries is the rigidity of their production structure, the product of their limited resource base, and specific soils and climate. Indeed, the most plausible explanation of the alleged historical tendency for the commodity terms of trade to run against them is in terms of the relative inflexibility of their response to altering market conditions. In some cases, as has been seen, foreign firms determine export volume on the basis of their world-wide interests, which are unlikely to be significantly affected by marginal policy changes in one country. There may also be longer-term problems in developing distribution and marketing systems which are themselves responsive to altering market opportunities. Furthermore, particularly where population growth is rapid, domestic consumption may eat up the growth in production of exportables.

In planning for the longer run, investment strategy must also allow for the possibility of high returns from further research and development in the field of production, as well as in the field of end-use which has already been mentioned. Supply curve shifts through the introduction of new seeds and production techniques have produced dramatic results in many agricultural exporting sectors, among which are natural rubber, sisal and cotton, each of which is under competitive pressure from synthetics. These cost reductions make it possible for the export sectors and economies concerned to improve their performance even in the face of deteriorating world prices and commodity terms of trade; they make possible, that is to say, improvements both in the single factoral terms of trade and in the income terms of trade. In some circumstances, technological progress may have acquired a momentum of its own and production of a particular commodity may already be expanding in a virtually 'uncontrolled' fashion. While this eventuality renders a 'finely tuned' supply strategy still more difficult, it is quite likely to be beneficial, all things considered, unless the exporting country is a major world supplier.

Relative importance of supply and demand factors

There has been considerable discussion recently as to whether supply or demand factors carry the principal responsibility for recent commodity export performance, whether good or unsatisfactory, in the developing areas. Since there does not appear to be any argument as to the *general* presence of the primary product demand constraints mentioned above, divergent export experience among developing countries must reflect either differences in specific product market characteristics or different experiences and policies on the supply side.

To the extent that developing countries as a group lost out as suppliers in total world *consumption* (or production), of any particular product, they could either have become less competitive or otherwise been constrained on the supply side, or they could have been excluded by more protective restrictions on imports imposed by the consuming countries. Research which might shed light on these questions has not been conducted. If their share of total *imports* of the developed world also fell, and if there have been no new preferential trading systems introduced, there is a presumption that their competitiveness has weakened relative to other foreign suppliers. For many, mainly temperate, competing agricultural commodities, developing countries' share of imports to rich countries *has* fallen in recent years. This was particularly true of cereals, oilseeds and vegetable oils. Half of these agricultural market losses, by value, were registered in the EEC, suggesting that the *new* reciprocal trade preferences within the EEC were in large part responsible. There is also, however, a significant (rank) correlation between the rate of growth of total industrial country imports of particular commodities and the size of the developing countries' loss of market share for these commodities, suggesting that supply bottlenecks in the developing countries also played a role (Cohen and Sisler, 1970; IMF–IBRD, 1968, p. 17). Thus in *some* instances, at least in the relatively short run, expansion in world demand for the products they produce may still leave poor countries with a diminishing share of world trade; the problem *can* be on the supply side. For those commodities in which poor countries are the sole suppliers nothing much of this sort can be said – their share of world imports obviously *must* remain the same. Corroborative evidence is offered by other empirical studies of the exports of samples of developing countries which have found that total *relative* export performance is correlated with factors other than the market performance of the 'traditional' primary products in which each country specialized (De Vries, 1967 and Kravis, 1970).

The results of these studies, while significant, do not alter the fact that poor countries' export performance is constrained by the world commodity demand factors described above. (These demand influences upon individual primary product markets are themselves undoubtedly correlated one with another). They suggest, rather, that, supply policies and difficulties, particularly with respect to the development of new exports, account in large part for country-to-country differences in export performance within those constraints.

Very broadly -

Demand.

Ag & food, the problem is the market (low elasticity, + substitutes) and their share (production)

While metals/oils the problem is profits share.

3 International Commodity Policies

Among the means of improving the prices and earnings of poor countries from the sale of their primary products are:

1. Removal of existing trade barriers imposed by more developed countries.

2. Expansion of trade among developing countries.

3. Co-ordinated management of the supplies of individual commodities and/or the negotiation of international commodity agreements.

Removal of trade barriers in developed-country markets

The removal of trade barriers to primary product exports from poor countries, or at least a standstill on existing ones, has been 'on the international agenda' for a good many years now. The GATT Programme of Action called, in 1963, among other things for a standstill on further tariff or non-tariff barriers to the exports of developing countries, elimination of quantitative restrictions and internal revenue duties – which do not protect anyone in the imposing countries – on imports from developing countries, and duty-free entry for tropical products, as well as including a commitment to reduce tariffs on processed and semi-processed products from less-developed countries. Since then, Part IV, a new chapter dealing with trade and development, has been added to the General Agreement on Tariffs and Trade (GATT), outlining the obligations of the developed members with respect to the earliest possible non-reciprocal reduction and elimination of barriers to products of export interest to less developed members and a standstill on the introduction of any further such trade barriers.

But a wide variety of import tariffs, excise duties, import

quotas, sanitary regulations, and other devices for the protection of producers in the developed nations still remain. About one third, by value, of all primary products exported from developing countries face such trade barriers. The burden which these barriers impose upon the primary producers varies greatly with the product and the country. Clearly, the problem is most acute in those instances in which there exist competing producers within the developed countries which are being asked to lower their barriers. Unfortunately, the list of primary commodities produced to a considerable extent in developed as well as underdeveloped nations is a long one – it includes sugar, rice, oilseeds, fats and oils, cotton, tobacco and all of the temperate foodstuffs, such as cereals, meat, dairy products, etc. Of the list of commodities in Table 5, only coffee, copra and jute are *entirely* produced in developing areas. There can therefore be little assurance that the relevant trade barriers in the developed countries will fall or that, if they do, they may not be resurrected. Perhaps a realistic objective would be merely to reserve *expansion* in developed-country markets to primary produce from developing areas so as to ease the adjustment problems of competing inefficient producers in the importing countries; in some key markets, notably sugar, protective policies are still actually *reducing* the more efficient poor nations' market shares. One calculation suggests that even such a relatively modest objective would raise import demand for sugar in the industrial countries by 15 per cent to 25 per cent within ten years (Maizels, 1968, p. 301; IMF–IBRD, 1968, pp. 28, 103).

There have been several attempts to measure the impact of these trade barriers upon the exporting countries. In principle, the measurement of the effect of an import tariff or excise duty upon the earnings of the producing countries is easy enough. In Figure 2, an import or excise duty levied at the rate of AB/BC lowers the demand curve facing exporters of the commodity in question from DD_d to DD_w, and thereby lowers the equilibrium price received by these exporters from OH to OG, and the volume of their sales from OE to OC. The foreign exchange earnings lost as a result of the tariff, then, are shown by $OHFE - OGBC$; the real income loss, however, is only the

Assuming that the factors represented by BFEC are re-employed elsewhere.

area *HFBG* since the area under the supply curve represents the real cost of producing the export, which has also been reduced.

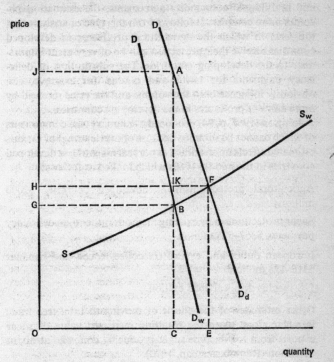

Figure 2

In order to produce the desired estimates, one requires some empirical information about the characteristics of the supply and demand curves in question. For some products this also requires knowledge of supply curves in the protecting countries. As mentioned earlier, there do now exist a number of estimates of elasticities of demand which are likely to be applicable to the range of prices in question. 'Guesstimates' must, however, be employed for the supply side. Thus it is possible to arrive at some rough estimates of the effects of removing tariff barriers upon the incomes of exporters. Where there exist quotas or, as in some cases, a variety of bilateral and multilateral commodity agreements, the estimation becomes more complex. It follows from this type of analysis that the *form* in which the agricultural producers in developed countries receive their protection can be of very great importance to the developing countries. The substitution of deficiency payments for tariffs and quotas, for example, can obviously influence both the volume and the price received by more efficient producers in the developing countries.

Johnson (1967, p. 94) produced a summary (the components of which cannot be summed because of overlapping) of various estimated effects upon annual export earnings of less developed countries in the middle-1960s which looked as follows:

Agricultural protectionism in developed countries $2000 million

Sugar protectionism by existing methods rather than deficiency payments $357–525 million

European duties and excises on coffee, cocoa and bananas $110–125 million

US surplus disposal $685 million

Other estimates of the effects of moving to total free trade in sugar alone place the resulting increased value of sugar exports from low-income sugar-producing countries at about $1 billion (Raquibuzzaman, 1970).

Decisions on the part of the socialist countries to admit more primary products from developing countries, i.e. to 'lower trade barriers', will be taken only as part of their total planning effort and will be implemented through instructions to their state trading agencies. When this expanded trade takes the form of a bilateral commodity exchange it is obviously necessary for the primary product exporter to calculate the implicit price from the terms of the commodities-for-commodities exchange in order to ascertain the value of the trade to his country relative to alternative market opportunities.

Expansion of trade with other developing countries

Only one-half of the primary-product imports of developing countries come at present from other developing countries. Excluding fuels, this proportion is only 36 per cent and is falling (calculated from UN *Monthly Bulletin of Statistics*). Rapid population growth, higher income-elasticities – and probably also price-elasticities – of demand for primary products characterize the poorer lands. There obviously exists considerable potential for the expansion of primary products trade, as well as the more frequently discussed trade in industrial products, among developing countries. There frequently exist institutional biases favouring the continuation of trading relationships between the poor nations and the rich at the expense of the trade ties which are officially sought among the developing countries themselves. This may be the case even with less developed country imports of primary products. The availability of credit for financing imports and exports is, for instance, usually greater in the traditional trading channels where there already exist specialized knowledge and institutions for the purpose. Traditional banking institutions, particularly where foreign-owned, may be unable or unwilling to develop new business arrangements of the required type. Payments regulations may also be biased against the development of new trade relationships among at least certain of the developing countries. Quality and regularity of supplies may also, at least until new trading links are established, favour importation from the industrial countries. Government assistance in the industrial countries may further deflect the trade in primary products from its 'normal' channels through surplus disposal programmes, special insurance schemes or concessional interest rates for export programmes, and tied aid. For this market potential to be realized, efforts will be required to develop new marketing channels and means of financing among the developing countries themselves.

International agreements

Price supports and stabilization

Attempts at international agreements to stabilize and/or support individual commodity prices have a long history. The interrelationships between price, or income, support objectives and stabilization objectives have not always been clear. 'Stabilization' has frequently simply served as a convenient euphemism for support – the fundamental issue manifesting itself as soon as the negotiations concerning the price range within which stability is to be sought begin. In the decade of sparring over the terms of an international cocoa agreement, for instance, the interest of the producers has varied directly, and that of the consumers inversely, with the world cocoa price, since the plausible price range for the agreement fluctuated with the cocoa market. The possible direct costs of export instability will be considered at greater length in chapter 5. It may be worth considering here, however, some of the possible interrelationships between commodity price stabilization and aggregate export producer earnings.

It is possible, though for policy purposes not very helpful, to derive the (static) elasticity conditions under which price stabilization will actually lower export revenues. But what are the underlying factors which ultimately matter? Price instability *may* reduce world demand for the commodity in question if the uncertainty which it produces as to the cost of inputs and the resultant holding of excess stocks, induces users, whether processors or final consumers, to switch to alternative products or even to invest in the development of synthetic or other alternatives. Synthetic substitutes are likely to carry a much more stable and therefore more certain price than the raw material, since the supplies are more subject to control; to the processor they also may have the advantage of being internal to the firm, constituting backward integration. Once developed, the existence of a synthetic is a highly stabilizing influence on the world raw commodity price, but this is likely to be small comfort to commodity producers if the stability is at a low price level and their market share is dwindling.

This same price uncertainty could restrict long-term supply capacity as well as demand, but domestic policies within the producing nations frequently insulate producers from at least some of this uncertainty, and price uncertainty is, in any case, often swamped by volume uncertainty so that the supply effects are more doubtful. Although there is as yet no firm empirical verification of this, there is therefore a reasonable presumption that international price stabilization will raise long-run demand *somewhat*. Progress with synthetics probably has a vigorous momentum of its own, however, and is likely to be more closely related to the levels of commodity prices than to their variability; the importance of this effect is therefore likely to be small.

Unstable world commodity prices will presumably induce some private consumers – dealers or processors – to hold larger stocks than otherwise. Price stabilization, by itself, would therefore create a once-for-all running down of these stocks to new lower levels, exerting a temporary dampening of world demand for the commodity in question. If the price stabilization is achieved through an internationally-operated buffer stock, the new authority may simply find itself taking over the formerly private stocks; to the extent that the producers contribute to its maintenance they may then have lost through its creation.

The impact of price instability on producers' earnings will also depend upon the skill with which national marketing is conducted. A stabilized price will be beneficial or prejudicial to the producing nation to the extent that its marketing was inept or skilful in the playing of a fluctuating market.

It should by now be evident that the issues relating to international commodity agreements are quite complex. The remainder of the discussion here will focus on the possibilities of using supply management and other related devices simply as instruments for raising or supporting commodity export prices at levels above those at which they would otherwise settle, and will leave the stabilization question for chapter 4.

Why. Surely they will be just as anxious (*not more so*) to avoid overstocking (or is this just a retail phenomenon?).

Supply restriction

The raising of the price for a commodity export would seem to constitute pure gain for the producing nations in that they incur no increased factor costs thereby, as they would for increased export volume, unless the product of extraordinary influences like perfect weather, and there are no restrictions on the use of the proceeds – as there would be, for instance, in the case of development assistance. Supply management to attain this outcome is obviously not, however, a simple matter.

Under what conditions should the exporters of a particular commodity co-ordinate their supplies so as to raise their joint welfare? The object of the exercise is to exert monopoly power through a cartel-like agreement to restrict supplies. It obviously pays to restrict world supplies when they exceed OQ_1 in Figure 3, since world demand is inelastic and the marginal revenue to producers as a whole is negative in that range. (The demand curve DD, and the supply curve SS, can be interpreted as relating either to the world market for the commodity in question, or to the supply and demand conditions facing one exporting country. Marginal revenue is shown by the schedule labelled MR.) Similarly, if a single nation faces inelastic world demand it pays it – with or without international agreement – to withhold supplies. This is a familiar maxim from the theory of the optimal tariff. But the supply side is also relevant, and unless the marginal costs of production are zero or negative it will pay still further to restrict supplies to OQ_2, where marginal revenue is equated with the marginal (social) cost of the commodity's production; thus supply restriction may be profitable to the producers or a single producer even when world demand for the commodity in the relevant range is price-elastic.

This seems a straightforward enough rule for the employment of supply management. One can collect existing econometric evidence on world price elasticities of demand and rapidly deduce which commodity markets should be managed and which not. Or can one? Apart from data imperfections and the paucity of demand studies, it is clear that the available observations cover a very limited range of possibilities. We simply do not know the elasticities for price and quantity ranges outside recent world experience. Even those data we do have are based on short-run observations: the response of demand to short-run price changes may be utterly different from that to secular price changes; in this context the already mentioned possibility of differential speeds in the development of synthetic substitutes or alternative sources of supply in response to price changes is a very real one. It must therefore be the long-run demand schedule which is relevant to the decision as to to whether to restrict or not. (Long-run elasticity

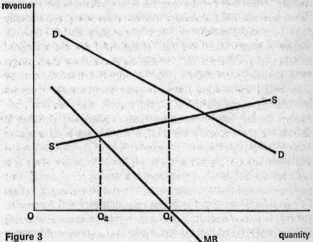

Figure 3

of demand, particularly where a synthetic is threatening, will be higher than the short-run one.) But that schedule is, of course, itself susceptible to change. In fact, the producing nations may themselves seek to change it through advertising, and promotion of new uses for the product and new markets. The relevant supply schedule is also the long-run one which reflects the costs of building new capacity.

Once the decision to seek to restrict supplies is taken, the question arises of how best to accomplish the restriction. And

So as always we want to know LRMC !!!
But we haven't a clue what it is!

now the international dimension of the scheme throws up some extra problems for the decision makers beyond those conventionally faced by domestic supply management arrangements. There exists no supranational authority which can order production to be curtailed in specific areas, assign production or sales quotas, impose export taxes, or otherwise *enforce* the necessary policies. Whatever device is arrived at for restricting supplies, it must be voluntarily agreed upon by all the producing nations, each of which has its own interest to pursue. A low-cost producing country with a small share of the world market is unlikely to be keenly interested in a supply restriction scheme which limits its right to increase its share of the market. Thus East Africa has been unenthusiastic about an international tea agreement. Small exporters may be able to count on the large exporters to restrict supplies and so support world prices even without their co-operation, as Brazil did for its coffee in an earlier period – at least until the market share of the small exporters has risen to the point where they have an interest in co-operative restriction. Yet without their co-operation the scheme cannot be wholly successful. Somehow a compromise must be struck. It may involve trading co-operation on one commodity in which supply restriction is not particularly in a country's interest for reciprocal co-operation on another commodity or issue in which it is.

The major difficulty with supply restriction schemes is that it is so difficult to avoid building considerable inefficiency into them; for the co-operative decision to withhold supplies is unlikely simply to produce movement back along the world supply schedule in Figure 3, with the highest-cost producers going out of production. This would only be the case if supply restriction could be achieved through a tax to be levied equally on all the producers, all of whose money costs were close approximations to social costs. The independent taxing, pricing and exchange rate powers of each separate government, however, renders such a tax impossible to enforce; governments would too easily offset – either consciously or unconsciously – the effects of the uniform tax, making it quite impractical as the sole instrument of supply restriction. The International Coffee Agreement has a 'diversification tax' which may indeed encourage each government so to restrict its supplies but it is the quota system and not the tax itself which is the ICA's instrument of supply restriction. This possibility nevertheless continues to receive attention.

The usual solution – 'the traditional method of supply management' – which has been employed in the cases of coffee, tea, sugar, tin and hard fibres, is to assign export quotas (rights) to the participating states. The only obvious formula for assigning such quotas is one based primarily on recent production or sales, with perhaps some extra weight given to recent rates of growth and/or readjustment. The likely outcome is thus that all producing states, whether low-cost or high-cost, will initially be asked to restrict supplies by roughly the same percentage – rather than the more efficient (from the world's point of view) solution of moving only the highest-cost producers out of production, with the 'losers' perhaps receiving some compensation from the 'gainers'. The difficulty with this, then, is that it tends to ossify existing international patterns of production, supporting inefficient producers at the expense of more efficient newcomers. Within each country, however, wise policies can still minimize these effects.

Difficulties of accommodating small new exporters are likely to be considerably mitigated in the happy circumstances of a rapid expansion in world demand. In their absence, acrimonious disputes over the periodic readjustment of quotas are virtually inevitable. One device which might be employed both to overcome some of these disputes and to improve efficiency would be to make the annual right to export, however determined, transferable at a price between countries; this, at any rate, would seem preferable to the phenomenon of restricted commodities travelling illegally between countries, as 'tourist coffee' did in the 1960s.

Once agreement is reached on the export quotas, the participating countries – and full participation by producers is an obvious essential for success – will be faced with the problem of restricting their own domestic production. While heavier taxes, lower prices, easy credit for diversification and so forth can be expected to have an impact on investment decisions, the variable costs of production, particularly in the case of peasant-produced tree crops, may be so low that it becomes extremely difficult to reduce production in the short run.

The problem of storage is then likely to arise. While world market supply management can be fairly finely tuned, even in the short run, simply through resort to stockpiling and/or destocking, the costs may be considerable. International agreements can vary in the assignation of responsibility for the stores and/or their financing. In the case of the International Coffee Agreement, each producing nation, once assigned its export quota, had to manage its own supplies, with the result that Brazil held at one point stocks equivalent to well over a year's supply, some of which eventually turned 'musty' in storage. World coffee stocks in 1967 amounted to the equivalent of about eighteen months worth of normal world consumption. The tin agreement, on the other hand, provides for international financing of a jointly-managed buffer stock as well. The IMF–World Bank Group has recently announced its willingness to assist in the financing of either nationally- or internationally-held commodity stocks, which are maintained in support of an international commodity agreement.

Apart from its usually being in the interest of the smallest participants to break the rules, there is clearly very great temptation for everyone else to breach the terms of the international agreement in order to save on storage costs or other unnecessary losses. What discipline can be exerted against the parties to an international supply restriction scheme to ensure compliance with their assigned export quotas? Evidently the threat of expulsion from the agreement would be of little force; those who break its terms are likely to be reluctant members. Unless they are prepared to consider retaliation in other spheres of economic or political policy, e.g. tariffs, import controls, votes at the UN, there is little which the other producers can do.

Effective policing can only be undertaken by the consumers who, if parties to the agreement, can simply refuse to accept commodities which are sold without the agreement's sanction.

The formal international 'rules of the game' for international commodity agreements, established by the GATT, require equal representation from consuming and producing nations and set a five-year limit to each agreement, but not all of the attempts to manipulate prices through international agreement have been constrained by these rules. These rules, in any case, seem a little naïve in retrospect; some of the fiercest disagreements over commodity schemes have been among producing nations, and the governments of the consuming nations, or the processors who advise them, have not always had the interest of the final consumers at heart. Experience with supply restriction schemes which have proceeded without the participation of the major consuming nations has so far been altogether disappointing. The most recent examples were the attempts of the Cocoa Producers' Alliance to hold the cocoa price up in late 1965, and the informal arrangements to withhold supplies of hard fibres in 1968–9.

By no means all commodities lend themselves easily to supply restriction schemes. In part, as has been seen, this is a matter simply of demand elasticities. It will not be possible to exert co-ordinated monopoly power where, because of the availability of alternative products or synthetic substitutes, the elasticity of world demand facing the developing countries is high. Thus a scheme for groundnuts would be impractical because of the variety of other oilseeds which are competitive in many of its end uses, and a scheme for natural rubber could founder on the availability of a cheap synthetic.

A supply management scheme will be simpler to manage, particularly if quotas have to be adjusted according to some pre-established rules, if the commodity is fairly homogeneous in quality, and if it can be stored with a minimum of deterioration or other cost. Commodities usually considered best to fit these various requirements are the tropical beverages coffee, tea and cocoa, and certain specialized foodstuffs like spices and sugar.

Once it is clear that consumer participation is essential for the success of a supply restriction scheme, it is easy to see why there have been so few successful schemes. The only major success story of recent years is the International Coffee Agreement which, it is estimated, has increased the export earnings of coffee producers by an average of $500,000 per year since 1962 when it first came into effect (IMF–IBRD, 1968, p. 123).

If, to be successful, consumer nations must co-operate in any supply restriction scheme, the object of which, it will be recalled, is to raise prices to themselves, i.e. reduce their real incomes, they may reasonably ask themselves if this is the optimal way in which to offer development assistance or to raise the earnings of the industry or countries in question. It distributes the burden oddly – to the consumers only – distributes the gains according to the quotas which may bear little relation to need or any other assistance criterion, and offers the donor a minimum of control over the use of the earnings. This last is one of its principal advantages to the recipients. An important advantage to the government of the consuming country may well be that, in this period of flagging public support for development assistance, it may enable it to achieve a resource transfer without its being visible as 'aid'; this has certain advantages for the producing countries as well, in most of which there is considerable sensitivity concerning the aid relationship.

Duty rebates

One possible alternative policy deserves particular attention. When the demand elasticity conditions for successful supply restriction seem to be met it may be administratively easier, though perhaps politically more difficult, for the consuming country to collect a consumption (or import) duty on the producers' behalf than to devise an international market regulation scheme. Where such taxes are already in existence there has been considerable clamour, in the GATT, UNCTAD and elsewhere, for their removal to assist the exporting countries. It may be relatively easy and preferable instead to earmark the revenues for development assistance – always provided that other development assistance is not cut by an equal amount!

In Figure 2 (see p. 49) DD is the demand curve the exporters face in the importing country in question when it levies an import duty at a rate of AB/BC. If the world supply curve to that country is SS_w, the world price available to exporters from sales in this country is BC, the domestic price in that country is AC, and the import duty is AB. Suppose now the duty is removed. The new domestic price, which is now equal to the world price, is EF. By assumption, the demand curve DD_d is inelastic; therefore $OHFE$, the new total take from the consumers, is less than $OJAC$, the former total take from consumers, despite the fact that the producer price has risen from OG to OH and producer earnings from $OGBC$ to $OHFE$. That is to say that, other things being equal, the producers would have been better off with the transfer of the duty revenues ($GJAB$) than with their removal. This case is strengthened to the extent that the supply curve is upward sloping, reflecting increasing factor costs, for then it is not the comparison between the revenue rectangles $OJAC$ and $OHFE$ which is relevant, but the producer surplus areas $GJAB$ and $GHFB$. The maintenance of the duty has the added advantage, to the producers of the commodity in question, of avoiding an increase in the effective protection offered to processors in the importing country which could otherwise be an undesirable by-product of duty removal (see chapters 4 and 8).

It has been estimated that the transfer of only 20 per cent of existing European fiscal revenues on tropical products would provide substantially greater earnings to the producing nations than would their total abolition (IMF–IBRD, 1968, p. 105). Denmark at present earmarks its coffee duty for development assistance, although there remain Danish controls over the resulting revenues. Canada rebates a duty on its sugar imports from the Caribbean to the governments of the producing countries; indeed, the latter governments protested vigorously when Canada attempted to replace this scheme with an increase in agricultural development assistance ostensibly of about five times the value. Some have advocated a system which would distribute the duty revenues on the basis of a formula which describes the extent of diversification out of the commodity in question in each producing country rather than automatically to the country of origin.

An analogous argument can be made for the imposition of a duty, where one did not exist before, as a means of raising commodity earnings. The object of the duty would then be to move the equilibrium point from F to B in Figure 2, raising the producer country's total revenues from $OHFE$ to $OJAC$ and, as we have seen, the producer country's real incomes by still more. To maximize the gain to exporting nations, the duty should be such as to reduce sales to the same degree as the optimizing supply-restricting agreement would. It would be the exporting country's reponsibility to ensure that the improved prices were not permitted to encourage further production. Reduced producer incomes in the exporting country, which should reduce supplies, are built into the scheme unless the government in that country feels it must pass on its duty revenues to the producers.

Besides lowering effective protection to processors and raising exporting countries' incomes (even if aid were reduced by an equivalent amount it would probably have carried more tying provisions so that the exporters would still be ahead), both of which objectives are also attained by supply-restricting agreements, this species of commodity agreement has four further advantages. Firstly, it can be implemented unilaterally by each importing country, without waiting for a tortuously negotiated international agreement which may, in fact, never be forthcoming; this would, however, require safeguards against a flood of new exporters coming and bidding away the gains available in the particular importing country paying the rebates. Secondly, it can be employed even in cases such as oilseeds where the complexity of any possible supply restricting scheme begins to boggle the mind. Thirdly, it provides, within itself, the encouragement to consumption within the poorer countries which supply-restricting schemes which raise overall prices do not, for only the rich would impose the duty upon their consumers. And finally, it can easily be imposed upon competing substitute products at the same time as it is imposed upon the imported material, thus reducing demand elasticity which might otherwise be buoyed by the availability of locally produced synthetic or other substitutes. The further fact that the revenues go directly to government rather than the producers may or may not be an advantage – no doubt it depends on the government – but it removes any presumption that higher world prices will make it more difficult to discourage production. A 'support-price' variant of this approach is the use of an import duty which, instead of remaining invariant, would vary according to the difference between an agreed reference price and the actual world price, the proceeds to be refunded to the producing countries.

Guaranteed minimum prices

Schemes for the international guarantee of certain *minimum* (support) prices – without necessarily any accompanying supply restrictions – are another possibility. International agreements to this end frequently provide for maximum prices as well, and are therefore said to be stabilization schemes, but the producers' interests are always firmly fixed upon the support price. Consuming countries have, on occasion, provided such guarantees for particular countries and commodities in the past. Both France and the UK offered bulk purchase contracts to their former colonies for several years at a time. France paid support prices for many of the commodity exports of its former colonies and, to some extent, the EEC still does. The Commonwealth Sugar Agreement and the US sugar quotas are further examples of the payment of prices above world market rates, although the latter are, in this case, themselves depressed by protective policies pursued by the consumer governments in favour of their own sugar beet interests. Many schemes combine a maximum and minimum price with export quotas adjustable on the basis of recent price behaviour. The International Grains Arrangements, formerly the International Wheat Agreement, although not of much assistance to developing countries, constituted a set of international *multilateral* contracts to buy and sell stipulated quantities at prestipulated minimum, and maximum, prices.

Co-operation against foreign firms

There are possibilities for successful co-operation among exporting countries, without the co-operation of consumers, in ways other than supply restriction. In the case of petroleum and mineral production, where, as has been seen, there is typically a high degree of market concentration in production, processing and marketing, international agreements among producing countries are likely to take a different form. The international firms already have achieved a certain degree of international market control so as to regularize volume and stabilize and raise the level of commodity prices. The 'solutions' thus arrived at may not, however, coincide with those which would be sought jointly by the host governments in the interest of the countries in which production is located. Conflicts between foreign resource-producing firms and host governments, acting either individually or collectively, are therefore likely and they may take many different forms. In this context they arise as conflicts over the 'division of total net revenues from operations between the foreign company and the host government'; and conflict over 'the control of export prices, output, and other conditions affecting the level of total revenues'. (Mikesell *et al.*, 1971, p. 30). Both have obvious international implications.

If one country extracts terms from a foreign mineral-producing firm which are more profitable for the host country than those in other actual or potential host countries, the firm may seek to shift its operations to such other countries, unless these other countries themselves alter the terms of their demands as well. Co-ordination among host countries as to the terms to be offered to foreign investors in the minerals industries – as to taxation arrangements, permissible repatriation of profits, posted prices, and so forth – may be the most effective form of international co-operation and market control. The object, in this case, is to secure, for the host countries jointly, the largest possible rent from the possession of the scarce mineral resources. Rather than directly restricting supplies, the host countries seek jointly to obtain improved prices

– meaning payments to government and other local factors –
from the foreign firms through bargaining in what amounts to
a bilateral monopoly situation. The success of the OPEC
(petroleum exporting) countries in extracting roughly 25 per
cent gains in tax revenues from the petroleum firms early in
1971 illustrates the possibilities when the timing is right,
although it will, unfortunately, raise import prices in many
poor countries as well as rich. The copper-producing countries
have a similar international organization (CIPEC) which may
soon seek similar successes. Far more difficult would be any
attempt of the OPEC or CIPEC countries to negotiate an
international commodity agreement which sought to regulate
supplies through assigned quotas and importers' co-operation.

4 Industrial Exports

Non-traditional or 'minor' exports have grown more rapidly than traditional exports from most developing countries in recent years. While new and minor primary products, and certain services like tourism, will undoubtedly continue to play an important role in the future export performance of most developing countries, it is the development of manufacturing for export around which most interest revolves and in which the greatest hopes are placed.

Exports of manufactured and semi-processed goods have been growing more rapidly, in the aggregate, than have exports of primary products from developing countries (see Table 4). From 7 per cent of total exports from developing countries in 1953, they have risen to over 20 per cent in 1969; their share in world trade in manufactured goods, however, has scarcely altered and still stood at 6·7 per cent in 1969.

What success there has been with manufactured exports in the Third World is highly concentrated: in 1969, 48 per cent of total manufactured exports came from Hong Kong, Taiwan, India and Yugoslavia, and 75 per cent came from only thirteen countries (these four, plus Israel, Mexico, Iran, Pakistan, South Korea, Philippines, Argentine, Brazil and Malaysia). Selected individual countries have been experiencing quite spectacular rates of export growth in this sphere in recent years. Taiwan's total exports, for instance, have been growing at about 20 per cent per year, and South Korea's by even greater proportions during the 1960s. In both cases, industrial exports have led the growth, accounting by 1968 for 66 per cent of Taiwan's exports and 74 per cent of South Korean exports (Sicat, 1969).

Measurement of industrial export development

The importance of export development can, for this purpose, be measured by the share of exports in total production, either globally, with respect only to the industrial (or any other) sector, or with respect to particular industries. The global export–GNP ratio is clearly not of much help to this type of analysis since it will be dominated by 'traditional' export and other activities. The export–production ratio for manufacturing industry and its components is, however, an extremely useful indicator of the type of industrial growth which is occurring. (Import-substituting industrialization will, obviously, register zero export development; other measures of import substitution will be discussed in chapter 6.)

An absolute measure of export development between periods t_0 and t_1 is

$$Q_t(x_t - x_0),$$

where x is the proportion of the value of production which is exported in period t, and Q_1 is the value of production in period t. (On grounds of symmetry with the conventional import substitution measures, there may be something to be said for using total supplies, imports plus domestic production, instead of Q_1). For comparisons as between industries and countries, a relative measure is required. One could employ a measure of the share of the increase in manufacturing production which is attributable to export development:

$$\frac{Q_1(x_1 - x_0)}{Q_1 - Q_0}$$

Alternatively, one might employ a measure of the relative increase in the extent of export development as follows:

$$\frac{x_1 - x_0}{x_0}$$

All of these measures would be substantially improved through the use of value added data in place of the production data.

Table 9 contains Pakistani data on x_t for a number of manufacturing industries, and shows the rapid export development over the decade 1954/5–1964/5 in many consumer-goods (and a few other) industries. Table 10 shows, for a sample of less developed countries, the growth in the value of manufac-

Table 9 **Per cent of industrial production exported, selected industries, Pakistan 1954/5–1964/5**

	1954/5	1964/5
Consumer goods	3·8	10·1
Of which		
Food mfg. n.e.c.	1·8	18·1
Cotton and other textiles	0·8	20·0
Footwear	n.a.	18·1
Wood and furniture	7·5	2·1
Soap, cosmetics, etc.	0·1	7·5
Intermediate goods	32·4	31·7
Of which		
Jute textiles	56·2	65·2
Leather mfg.	86·6	76·2
Rubber products	0·1	6·7
Chemicals	10·3	7·1
Investment and related goods	2·2	2·4
Of which		
Machinery	7·1	6·5
Electric machinery and goods	1·2	3·1
Transport equipment	6·4	2·8

Source: Lewis (1970, p. 118).

tured exports as a proportion of the total increase in the value of manufacturing production, i.e.

$$\frac{Qx_1 - Q_0x_0.}{Q_1 - Q_0}$$

Only a very few poor countries have exports accounting for over 10 per cent of the expansion in the value of industrial production.

What accounts for these individual 'success' stories, and what are the future prospects for manufactured exports from the Third World? It may be worth distinguishing the relevant factors as between those having to do with demand and those relating to the supply side.

Table 10 Per cent of increases in industrial production which are exported, selected countries, early 1950s to mid-1960s[1]

Argentina	2	Mexico	14
Brazil	2	Nigeria	3
Burma	4	Pakistan	19
Ceylon	2	Panama	0
Colombia	3	Peru	0
Dominican Republic	4	Philippines	8
Honduras	3	Syria	10
India	4	Taiwan	44
Kenya	5	Thailand	6
South Korea	19	UAR	10

1. For details as to years covered and sources for primary data, see the original source.
Source: Kravis (1970, p. 179).

Demand problems

The income-elasticity of demand for manufactured products is, in the aggregate, believed to be higher than that for primary products; but there is likely to be very wide variation from commodity to commodity. Processed foodstuffs undoubtedly exhibit lower income-elasticity of demand, for instance, than do most metal-using products.

Of fundamental importance to the issue of Third World manufacturing export prospects are the barriers which are erected by the developed countries to restrict entry of these products to their own markets. Tariffs, quotas and other barriers in the markets of the rich constitute a major impediment to large-scale industrial exports. The tariff structures of the rich nations are such as to offer the greatest degree of effective protection (see chapter 8) to their producers in the very industries in which poor countries are most likely to be competitive – light industries relatively intensive in the use of unskilled labour such as textiles, footwear, rugs, sporting goods, handbags, processed foodstuffs, etc. This is precisely because of these industries' inability freely to compete, unskilled labour-intensity putting them at a comparative disadvantage within the context of their relatively high-wage economies.

These tariff structures are also biased against the further processing of primary products by primary product exporters, in that heavier duties are imposed in the importing countries, the higher the degree of processing. Thus, while the US import tariff on raw hides and skins is zero, its tariff on finished leather is 10 per cent and on leather footwear it is 13 per cent. Similarly with cocoa beans, cocoa butter, chocolate, copper, copper bars, etc. This 'escalation' or 'cascading' in the tariff, together with the relatively low proportion of value added in the early stages of processing, produces the very high rates of effective protection recorded in Table 11 (See discussion in chapter 8).

Tariff reductions bargained out within the GATT have not, in general, been of much use to exporters of manufactured goods from developing countries. Since these tariff reductions are, in accordance with the GATT norms, extended to all GATT members in a non-discriminatory fashion, it pays a country to bargain only with the dominant supplier of any particular commodity; it follows from the small share of developing countries in the manufactured imports of the rich countries that most of the tariff reductions will therefore be bargained out among the rich, any benefits to the poor arising only as incidental throw-offs from the original bargains. This pattern was not substantially altered in the most recent (Kennedy) round of tariff reductions (see Table 11). Where, as in the case of textiles and light labour-intensive industries, the rich nations *all* are relatively inefficient, they will each be unwilling to lower protection *vis-à-vis* one another lest they be swamped by further imports from the Third World, and *vis-à-vis* the Third World because the compensating benefits which the latter can offer are limited. The combination of the principles of non-discrimination and reciprocity has made the conventional GATT tariff negotiation system of limited

Table 11 **Averages of nominal and effective tariffs on industrial countries' imports of manufactures before and after the Kennedy Round**

	Nominal		Effective	
	Total imports	Imports from LDCs	Total imports	Imports from LDCs
	%	%	%	%
Pre-Kennedy	10·9	17·1	19·2	33·4
Post-Kennedy	6·5	11·8	11·1	22·6

Source: Little, Scitovsky and Scott (1970, p. 273).

relevance to the export prospects of manufacturing industries in developing countries.

As if these high rates of effective tariff protection were not enough, physical quotas are also employed to restrict entry of particularly troublesome manufactured items such as cotton textiles, clothing and processed agricultural products. The textile industry is traditionally one of the earliest to appear in any industrialization effort because of its unskilled labour-intensity, locally available raw materials, limited scale economies and sizeable local markets; in recent years between 30 per cent and 40 per cent of total Third World manufactured exports have been textile products. As competition from the Third World began to make inroads upon the textile markets of the developed world, the rich nations first attempted to persuade the new cotton textile exporters to impose 'voluntary' export quotas and finally resorted, themselves, to internationally-authorized import quotas under the terms of the Long-Term International Cotton Textiles Arrangements. These arrangements, originally negotiated in 1962, and subsequently extended, obligate each textile importing nation to admit at least a stipulated minimum annual increase in the volume of its textile imports from developing areas, unless these imports create 'market disruption'. 'Market disruption' is defined by the importing nation without international review and its presence entitles the nation which encounters it to impose quotas again restricting imports to their previous levels.

Predictably, with so liberal an escape clause, the 'minimum' increase was frequently taken by the importers as the maximum. It also authorizes the continued use of 'voluntary' export quotas which are frequently 'encouraged' by the importing industrial nations through threats to exporters of worse – and internationally permissible – measures. This agreement breaches the GATT principle of non-discrimination and also contravenes its usual norms with respect to the avoidance of quantitative restrictions.

Physical import quotas, 'voluntary' (but truly mandatory) export quotas, variable import levies, and anti-dumping duties, also restrict imports of other semi-processed and processed agricultural products from developing countries; recent cases of the last-mentioned type included the US response to Brazilian penetration of its instant coffee market and expanded sales of tinned mushrooms from Taiwan. Other so-called 'non-tariff barriers' – sanitary and safety regulations, public procurement policies, domestic-content regulations, border delays, etc. – impede still further the Third World's access to the rich nations' markets. Increasing attention has been devoted in recent years to these non-tariff barriers to international trade as successive rounds of tariff reductions under the auspices of the GATT are successfully concluded among the developed countries. There exists a certain amount of evidence to suggest that the non-tariff measures applied by advanced countries, like their tariffs, may be systematically biased against the exports of the poor (Walter, 1971).

It should hardly be surprising that the Third World countries have long been pressing for the relaxation of these many restrictions on their industrial export markets. Nor should it be surprising that they should turn inwards in their market orientation – to other Third World nations or, more commonly, to their own, often very small, domestic markets.

In Part IV of the GATT, which was adopted in 1964, its signatories agreed in principle that reciprocity in tariff negotiations with developing countries was to be abandoned. In the second UNCTAD in New Delhi in 1968 agreement was also reached on the desirability of introducing a multilateral non-reciprocal tariff preference scheme to favour semi-processed and processed products from developing countries in the markets of the rich – apparently another, more equitable, major breach of the basic GATT principle of non-discrimination in trade. In October 1970, agreement in principle on the schemes was achieved with the details to be worked out and implemented separately by each industrial nation on its own. There will be severe limitations, however, on its usefulness to the poor nations. Many of the most important processed products, from the Third World's viewpoint, involve the 'exceptional and compelling circumstances', from the viewpoint of the developed countries, which are required for their exclusion from the scheme. Thus processed agricultural foodstuffs were excluded from discussion of the scheme even in the New Delhi meetings, while cotton textiles were recognized from the outset as a 'special case'. These two categories make up nearly half of present manufactured exports from developing countries.

There have been many problems to resolve for those products which remain on the list of potential beneficiaries of this preference scheme. Are all developing countries to be considered equally or will the least industrialized (or otherwise least developed) receive special consideration? Will all products on the list receive equivalent preferences or will the provisions have to be negotiated for each product, item by item? For how long will preferences be offered and what provisions will there be for their renewal? How will the place of origin of processed products which are supposed to emanate from developing countries be defined so as to avoid the diversion of 'normal' trade in manufactures among industrial countries through developing countries simply to appropriate the preferences? How liberal will the inevitable escape clauses be? How will those developing countries now enjoying preferences be compensated for their losses?

It is already evident that these preferential arrangements are and will be quite limited in their original application, and it appears inevitable that the cotton textile arrangements will continue to be renegotiated in more or less their present restrictive form. What else can be hoped for on the demand side of the market for manufactures from developing countries? Probably the best hopes lie in the gradual introduction of improved adjustment assistance programmes in the developed world, which will enable the rich countries to adapt their economies – in their own self-interest! – to the industrialization of the Third World without undue hardship to particular groups, and without which protective trade barriers cannot realistically be expected ever to fall. Studies suggest that the overall cost of such readjustment programmes, particularly when compared with other costs of economic growth, would be very small. It has been estimated, using fixed labour coefficient data on projected output volume changes, that even a substantial increase in the rate of growth of the industrial countries' manufactured imports from the developing countries would produce employment effects in the affected industries which are well below the normal rates of labour turnover (Little, Scitovsky and Scott, 1970, pp. 285–9).

In the more immediate future, the developing countries might benefit from unilateral single-country concessions on products of interest to them, beyond those required to meet the international 'rules of the game', such as Australia offered a few years ago. A move to linear (across-the-board) tariff reductions in the next rounds of GATT bargaining would also reduce the bias against the poorest countries in international tariff-cutting.

Supply problems

On the supply side, there remain great difficulties of developing a capacity to export industrial products even if the market prospects were excellent. The wide divergence of experience with manufactured exports in the face of virtually identical market prospects suggests that supply considerations do play an extremely important role. (It does not prove, as some imply, that they are more important than demand factors in assessing overall future prospects for industrial exports.)

Poverty, of course, implies shortages of the industrial infrastructure, skills and experience which are required for successful industrialization efforts. The least developed countries of the Third World, notably those of tropical Africa, are at a serious disadvantage relative to such semi-industrialized countries as Argentina, Mexico and Brazil; this is demonstrated by the former's failure to develop industrial exports to Europe to any significant degree despite their preferential access to the British and/or European markets. Thus the supply response in the Third World to any improvement in market access will vary considerably from country to country. Even the semi-industrialized countries have difficulty, however, developing marketing facilities and contacts, arranging competitive trade financing, and generally keeping up with the markets in the industrial countries.

Apart from the further processing of their own raw material exports, it has been hypothesized that countries do not generally embark on the export of manufactured goods 'from scratch'. They normally first produce for domestic markets. This is certainly supported by the recent experience of Pakistan (Lewis, 1970, p. 117). This would place small countries at something of a manufacturing disadvantage at the outset – a hypothesis confirmed by the significant positive cross-sectional correlation between country size and both the share of manufactured goods in total exports and the share of finished as opposed to semi-finished goods in total manufactured exports (Balassa, 1969). Smaller countries – a category within which most of the Third World fits – are likely therefore to be comparatively successful at the export of standardized semi-manufactured goods and weak in the development of finished and differentiated manufactures. It is noteworthy that while per capita income does not appear to be significantly correlated with manufactured export success *within* the Third World, there does seem to exist an income 'threshold' across which a country must pass in order to become a potential manufacturing exporter.

The operations of the modern multinational corporation may, however, be rendering even these empirical generalizations obsolete. A new phenomenon of rapidly increasing importance is the 'putting out' to developing countries of unskilled labour-intensive processes, 'midway' in the production process, by international vertically-integrated corporations. Data are sent by air from New York to the West Indies to be punched on computer tape by relatively cheap labour, following which they are sent back again by air. Components of complex electronic equipment are manufactured in Taiwan, Hong Kong, South Korea and on the Mexican border with the US. In some instances these processes consist of components manufactured from local materials; in others they involve further processing of imported inputs which are then re-exported. It may well be that in such 'processes' rather than in 'industries', as conventionally thought of, lies the immediate industrial exporting future of the Third World; but export enclaves could develop, within which multinational firms purchase cheap labour and outside of which little impact is registered – 'outposts' of the 'mother countries' again. The prospects for this type of development depend, in large part, upon the tax treatment by the developed countries of these manufactured imports. As long as import duties are levied only upon the foreign value added and are kept low they should be bright. The multinational firms engaged in these activities will, for the first time, act as strong interest groups in the markets of the rich for liberal tariff policies such as these.

Ultimately the success of any effort to build an industrial exporting capacity will depend upon the incentives which exist for doing so. In part, and this is beyond the potential exporter's control, this is a matter of demand prospects. In large part, however, it is a matter of conscious domestic commercial and exchange rate policies, which are the subject of other chapters of this book. Suffice it to say, at this point, that most newly industrializing countries have offered few incentives to develop industrial exports. Industrialization efforts have concentrated far more upon substitution, through domestic production, of manufactured imports.

5 The Export Instability Problem

The instability of the exports of developing countries has been discussed and lamented for many years in the general literature of economic development. It is only relatively recently, however, that detailed empirical research has been undertaken, illuminating its causes and costs.

The level of domestic aggregate demand is not generally believed to be as important a determinant, in the short run, of the level of aggregate economic activity in the typical poor country straining against supply bottlenecks for the most rapid possible development as it is in the industrial economies. Rather, the level of income is considered to be supply-determined; despite the presence of substantial and obvious unemployment, most poor economies are considered to be in a state of (Keynesian) quasi-full employment. To the extent that demand factors play a major role in the short-term determination of the level of income, they are those emanating from the export sector rather than from domestic investment. Fluctuations in export demand, moreover, typically affect the aggregate level of income through their effects upon the level of foreign exchange earnings and thus upon available supplies, rather than through orthodox income-increasing multiplier (demand) effects. Supply fluctuations, engendered by such factors as weather, crop pests and diseases, are usually, however, at least as important as any demand factors in determining the short-term level of income and welfare, particularly in those economies in which agriculture still predominates. A discussion of export instability, then, must be placed in the context of economies with these characteristics with respect to overall instability.

The measurement of export instability is itself subject to a great deal of variation. Measures which have been employed range from relatively simple ones such as the average percentage annual change, to more sophisticated measures such as the standard error of a loglinear time trend fitted to annual observations divided by the mean of the observations. Virtually all of the empirical studies of export instability have employed annual data although it is not obvious that these are the most useful to employ, since they conceal fluctuations of either a longer-term or shorter-term nature whose policy importance may be at least as great.

Although there exist some time periods during which the exports of developing countries were not significantly more unstable than those of developed countries, it is now generally agreed that export prices, quantities and total earnings are all more unstable in the average poor country than in the average rich one. There is also evidence that, per capita income apart, small countries, of which there are many in Africa and Latin America, suffer greater export instability than large countries (Erb and Schiavo-Campo, 1969; Massell, 1970). Table 12 shows developing country export prices, volumes and earnings over the 1950–65 period to be roughly twice as unstable as those of industrial countries. Other studies, using different instability measures and different time periods, confirm this picture. The dispersion about the average is also considerably greater for the poor countries' group than for that of the rich, indicating that there exist some poor countries with a *very* high degree of export instability.

It is well to bear in mind, in this discussion, the distinction between the instability of exports, of all commodities, from particular developing *countries* and the instability of exports, from all developing countries, of particular *commodities*. When looking at individual country cases, one will obviously have to be concerned with the individual commodity cases which together make up that particular country's export bundle. One must also be clear as to which type of export instability it is which is to be discussed – instability in export prices, export volumes, or export proceeds, i.e. price times volume. One might also be interested in the instability of import prices faced by developing countries, but since fluctuations therein are generally less severe and, in any case, uncorrelated with any of the export variables with which we shall be concerned, no further consideration will be given to this aspect of the instability issue here.

Which is more unstable – export prices or export volumes – obviously depends on the country or the commodity and the

Table 12 **Exports from industrial and developing countries: average fluctuation indices and dispersion around the average, 1950–65 and 1953–65**

| | Average of fluctuation indices[1] | | Dispersion around the average[2] | |
	1950–65	1953–65	1950–65	1953–65
Industrial countries	%	%	%	%
Prices	3·7	2·1	1·1	0·6
Quantities	5·6	4·5	2·7	3·3
Earnings	6·2	4·2	2·1	1·6
Developing countries				
Prices	8·8	6·8	3·1	2·8
Quantities	9·5	8·0	8·4	4·5
Earnings	11·8	9·6	7·1	6·1

1. The fluctuation index employed is the average annual percentage deviation, neglecting sign, from the trend, which is estimated by fitting a linear relation between time and the logarithms of the annual observations.
2. Standard deviation from the mean.
Source: IMF – IBRD (1969, pp. 41, 59).

time period in question. The matter is further complicated by the fact that volume fluctuations themselves are likely to produce (offsetting) price fluctuations, other things being equal. In general, volume instability is rather more important in poor countries than one might expect from simply having considered the theoretical and institutional literature on stabilization, which devotes the bulk of its attention to price instability. What emerges from a number of empirical studies is that, for individual poor countries, export volume instability has, on average, exceeded export price instability during the post-1945 period. As far as primary commodities are concerned, total export volumes were, on average, more unstable than price in studies of the 1901–51 and 1953–65 periods, although not in the evidence for 1960–65 and 1946–58, no doubt because of the Korean War boom. All of the studies, without exception, show for both countries and commodities greater average instability of total export earnings than of either export prices or export volumes (UN, 1952; UNCTAD, 1968; Coppock, 1962; IMF–IBRD, 1968).

Causes of export instability
Volume

What lies at the root of the poor countries' high average degree of export instability? On the supply (volume) side, individual agricultural commodities are obviously subject to the possibilities of droughts, excess rainfall and floods, plant diseases and insect and other pests. While on the world market, variations in national crop conditions will, to some extent, mutually offset one another, the impact of such supply variations may be *very* great in individual producing countries. Tree crops, which have a gestation period of several years, may also be subject to a price–volume cobweb cycle, with volume changes induced by price changes of some years previously producing further price changes in the opposite direction which themselves affect volume again with a lag, and so on *ad infinitum*. It is a little more difficult to provide a general explanation of the fluctuations in export volume of some of the mineral products. The total volume of world exports in the well-managed petroleum industry is far more stable than its nearest rival commodity; but even petroleum export volume can be highly variable in particular producing countries. Apart from 'normal' market responses, strikes and political disturbances also play important roles. Of twelve underdeveloped countries singled out in one study as having suffered 'excessive' fluctuations in export earnings in the 1946–58 period, seven (Argentine, Iran, Korea, Vietnam, Indonesia, Iraq, Malaysia) could attribute a considerable share of the blame to 'political' factors or war (MacBean, 1966, p. 55).

Price

As far as export price fluctuations are concerned, one must distinguish between primarily demand-induced and primarily supply-induced fluctuations. As was argued before, the price-elasticity of demand for many primary products on world markets is low. Short-run supply elasticity in the producing countries is also typically fairly low, since at least in the case of agricultural commodities, once a crop is planted – especially in the case of tree crops which do not mature for several years – there is little scope for altering output except to the limited extent that the intensity of harvesting may vary. Even in the case of minerals, fixed costs typically make up a high proportion of the total, making it advantageous to operate at capacity for a very wide range of prices. It follows that relatively modest shifts in world demand or supply can have dramatic effects upon price.

The business cycle in the industrial countries produces cyclical variations in world demand for primary products and thereby exerts a major influence upon world commodity prices. When income-elasticities of demand are low, as in the case of most agricultural products, so is supply elasticity; when supply elasticity is a little greater, as in the case of metals, so is income-elasticity of demand. It was therefore once affirmed that the cure of the business cycle would overcome the commodity price instability problem. The relatively stable business conditions of the last two decades do appear to have damped price fluctuations somewhat, particularly for metals and agricultural raw materials, for which demand fluctuations are most important; but considerable demand-induced fluctuations remain, attributable in large part to the still quite violent fluctuations in inventory demands. Short-run shifts in world demand can also be generated by factors other than business conditions. Changes in the prices of competing goods, including synthetics, for instance, can have substantial impact upon world demand conditions.

Price fluctuations are also, of course, engendered by the very world volume fluctuations which are themselves a major source of export instability in producing countries. This is particularly so for tropical foodstuffs and beverages. Unless the price-elasticity of world demand is less (neglecting sign) than 0·5, in which case the extreme price fluctuations more than offset the volume fluctuations, these supply-induced price fluctuations tend to moderate the effects of volume variations upon world export earnings from the commodity in question: when supplies fall, the price rises, and conversely.

What is true for the world market may not, however, be true for the individual exporting nation. The world price variation which is the product only of *other* producers' supply instability may moderate *their* earning instability, but it constitutes just another source of price instability and therefore earning instability for any single exporter. For him, this supply-induced price instability is best regarded as demand-induced, the 'demand' in this case referring not to total world demand but to the demand for this country's exports of the commodity, *net* of the supply made available from the rest of the world. (Developed countries frequently supply themselves; the more they do so, frequently behind protective barriers, the more 'residual' and narrower – and therefore the more unstable – become the markets on which primary exporters must sell.) The demand schedule facing an individual producer of a particular commodity is thus not only differently shaped from that for the commodity on the world market, but is also subject to different shifts.

Export supply variations within a single producing country can be expected to produce offsetting world price changes unless, and this is commonly the case, its market share is so small that the world demand facing it is infinitely elastic. The impact of one's own export supply variation upon export earnings thus depends not only upon the world elasticity of demand for the export commodity in question but also upon one's own share in the world market. Generally, the smaller the market share the higher is the elasticity of net world demand facing the single exporting country and therefore the greater will be the export earnings fluctuations generated by export supply variations. Export earning instability with respect to one commodity and one country is thus most unlikely to exceed volume instability unless, as *is* normally the case, external demand (or others' supply) effects are also operative and important. The complexity of all of these interrelationships and the difficulty of assigning 'blame' for price and earnings fluctuations should by now be obvious.

Concentration

We can now move from the level of individual commodities to that of total exports from individual nations. It has long been believed that important influences upon a nation's export price, volume and earning instability are the degree of commodity concentration and, a little less plausibly, the degree of geographic concentration of export trade. It seems reasonable to postulate that the variations in supply, price and earnings of various commodities (and markets) will not be perfectly correlated one with another. It follows that diversification will reduce aggregate instability and uncertainty. A number of simple empirical tests of this seemingly obvious proposition did not, however, prove very conclusive (Coppock, 1962; Michaely, 1962; MacBean, 1966; Massell, 1964). One can easily think of reasons why. The particular commodities in the bundle are clearly of great importance; from the point of view of export price stability, for example, it matters a great deal whether one is highly concentrated in the export of gold or of copper! The share of food in total exports was found to be significantly negatively correlated with export earning instability in one recent econometric study (Massell, 1970). Moreover, supply or demand influences are more highly correlated in some export combinations than in others: one illustrative study has shown that, from the point of view of export price stability, the combination of copra and ground-nuts is far better than that of maize and cotton. The correlation coefficient between the world prices of the former pair was -0.47, whereas that for the latter was $+0.94$ (Brainard and Cooper, 1968, p. 272).

Analogous arguments could be made concerning the geographic 'bundle' of exports; in this case the statistical results, indicating an unexpected negative correlation between export instability and an index of geographical concentration, probably reflect the special trade relationships between former colonies and their metropoles. When such other influences are allowed for, export commodity concentration emerges, in accordance with common sense, as significantly correlated with export instability (Massell, 1970).

The costs of export instability

Is it unstable export prices or unstable export earnings that is the problem for developing countries to which international policy-makers should address themselves? (Presumably there is little they can do about unstable volume.) What exactly is the problem of instability? While export *price* uncertainty has certain costs, as will be seen, it is the instability of national export *earnings* which really matters.

The cost of export instability is, above all, that of carrying sufficient foreign exchange reserves or borrowing enough to enable the economy to ride relatively smoothly through the export fluctuations. The relative size of exports in total GNP will obviously be a major determinant of this cost. How important exports are relative to GNP varies greatly, and is not significantly correlated, at least statistically speaking, with per capita income; as the examples of India, China, Pakistan, Indonesia and Brazil would suggest, the share of exports in GNP is negatively correlated with country size, i.e. population (see chapter 1). This cost – taking the form of interest or superior earning opportunities forgone through the holding of extra inventories of foreign exchange reserves – is incurred even if the size and pattern of the instability is foreseen and completely predictable; it is obviously greater when the magnitude and direction of fluctuations are unknown. While the holding or borrowing of foreign exchange in 'sufficient' quantities sets the upper limit to the cost of export instability, it is worth considering what its costs would be if the economy were not thus smoothed.

The impact of export instability

It is necessary, first of all, to ascertain who bears the brunt of the fluctuations in export earnings. In some instances GNP may fluctuate relatively little in response to marked export fluctuations; a foreign-owned mine or estate may absorb in its repatriated profits and its inventories the annual ups and downs of the world market, leaving its employment, wage bill and fixed capital formation unaffected. GNP then fluctuates far less than GDP. There is evidence that Chilean foreign-owned copper mines have behaved in this way in the past (Reynolds, 1963; MacBean, 1966, p. 88). Where there are smallholder-produced agricultural exports, there also frequently exist government marketing boards which absorb much of the world price fluctuations in their reserves and pay the producers a stabilized price. Where such Boards do not exist, the bulk of the instability is probably felt directly by the farmer, although traders and middlemen may absorb some of it. Government fiscal policy obviously can also consciously offset the impact of export fluctuations, within the constraint of the availability of reserves, if government so chooses. Thus the domestic impact of export instability depends, among other factors, upon the nature of the product, market organization and the fiscal system.

To the extent that government revenues in poor countries come very largely from taxes on foreign trade and on the export sector, public revenues may be particularly disrupted by volatile export earnings, making it difficult to plan public capital formation programmes; where foreign-owned firms absorb much of the instability themselves, leaving the domestic private sector largely unaffected, government revenues – particularly profits taxes – may still be extremely volatile. Where the state is the major actor in the development effort and reserves are inadequate for it to proceed with its programmes smoothly in the face of revenue instability, it may even be desirable, if it is politically possible, to pursue an 'ultra-orthodox' fiscal policy of varying its revenue demands inversely with export earnings, thereby transferring most of the instability to the private sector, or, if possible, that portion of it which contributes least to development. Disrupted and uncertain public services and development programmes are a major cost of export instability.

In the private sector, instability is likely to involve considerable economic and social costs. These will be felt not only in the export industry which will presumably bear the direct, or primary, impact – its degree depending on the extent to which such 'built-in stabilizers' as were mentioned above are operative, the importance of export earnings in the total income of those in the industry, and their capacity to shift out of exports into other economic activity – but also in the rest of the economy. To the extent that income recipients spend on domestic goods and services rather than on imports – in many poor economies this extent may be quite small – there will be secondary (multiplier) effects on prices and money incomes, if not on production, in other parts of the private sector, which will again have further implications for government revenues.

There will also be less direct effects on some sectors operating from the supply side. Many industries are dependent upon imports for key intermediate inputs, fuel and spare parts. If exchange or import controls are imposed in the difficult export periods, slowing down the flow of these imports or cutting them off entirely, and if they do not hold large inventories of them, these industries cannot produce at capacity. If possible, cutbacks of imports in times of export troubles will be confined to non-essential consumer-goods. Where, as in many Latin American countries, import substitution programmes have already taken the consumer-goods 'fat' out of the import bill (see chapter 6), there is no option, in these circumstances, but to cut back on imports which are 'essential' either for industrial production or for the development programme.

Nature of instability costs

Export instability can thus impart instability and its costs to a variety of sectors throughout the economy. These costs of instability can be summarized under the following headings:

(1) inherent social costs, (2) distortion of investment patterns, and (3) excess frictional costs.

1. Instability and uncertainty – they are not the same – of real, and perhaps money, incomes or employment levels are regarded by most individuals and by society as inherently undesirable. (Subsequent discussion will abstract from domestic price changes which will, of course, also affect the degree and pattern of income instability.) These fluctuations and uncertainty are likely to be a source of social disruption, further intensified by the instability with respect to income distribution to which they give rise, and a 'feast-or-famine' cast to society. While many will happily trade some income stability or certainty for higher average income – indeed, the decision to engage in international trade contains elements of such a trade-off – they would prefer that their incomes were high *and* stable, or at least less uncertain.

2. Risk aversion and/or instability aversion will lead investors and other decision-makers, whether subsistence farmers or industrialists, to engage less in the activities which are most subject to these factors than their (private or social) profitability alone would demand. The risk or instability faced by a domestic individual decision-maker or even by an entire industry is likely to be greater than that facing a nation, since the nation typically has or is capable of having many other 'eggs in other baskets'. On the other hand, there are social costs to local instability which a private decision-maker may not weigh, particularly if he is a large multi-national firm. The resulting discrepancy between private and social risk or instability aversion at the micro-level may, other things being equal, produce socially undesirable distortions in the overall patterns of economic activity. In the agricultural sector, for instance, it may discourage specialization and the movement from subsistence into the market economy.

3. Instability and uncertainty may also give rise to excess investment in boom periods, excess retrenchment in slack ones and a consequent wastage in scarce capital. (Total capital formation may, however, be increased through this mechanism.) Con-

struction begun on the upswing may be abandoned and left to deteriorate rapidly on the downswing. This may be the product either of altered expectations or, as has been seen, of inability to purchase key imported inputs. Similarly, the tree crops planted in the boom will not be tended and may even be uprooted in the recession. While there are always frictional costs for society in re-allocating resources, those from attempts, as export incomes fluctuate, to 'keep up', whether they are responses to relative price change or to changing availability of funds or key inputs, are likely to be excessive.

Other possible consequences of export instability which have been suggested include the reduction of savings rates and the creation of inflationary pressure, but the arguments for neither are convincing. At least as plausible as the argument that instability and uncertainty discourage private savings and investment is one that says that they will encourage individuals and firms to carry 'reserves' which are larger than otherwise, thus releasing resources which can be directed into productive channels through suitable monetary and fiscal policy. It can also be argued that excess investment generated during the optimism of booms exceeds the cutbacks in recessions – that there is a ratchet in savings or investment behaviour. (A ratchet in recurrent government expenditures could, of course, offset this.) All of this must remain somewhat speculative; the arguments would, in any case, have different applicability to different types of economy.

There exist a variety of different theoretical explanations of why export instability may generate inflation. These include: a ratchet preventing price reductions following boom-induced demand inflation, a ratchet effect in government expenditures which rise in response to increased revenues in the upswing but do not fall in the downswing, higher marginal propensity to spend of the rural sector for income increases than for decreases, and cost-push inflation produced by import constraints on downswings. These too are quite speculative and are not firmly supported by the empirical evidence (MacBean, 1966, p. 116; Argy, 1970, p. 76).

All of this discussion of costs has related to export earnings rather than to export prices. Instability or uncertainty of export *prices*, by themselves, can produce sub-optimal allocation of investment and the frictional costs incurred in too frequent reallocations through the mechanisms described above. Whether it is price or earnings which determines investment behaviour is a matter of fact, but one on which there is very little empirical evidence; the issue is analogous to the argument as to whether investment in an industrial economy is related to the profit rate or to 'residual funds'. With the exception of these effects on allocation decisions, export price instability is harmful to the domestic economy only through its contribution to export earning instability; where weather and pests are not contributors to export instability, price instability is likely to be the major cause of earnings variation. To the extent that export instability is a problem demanding international or domestic policy measures, they should therefore be primarily directed to smoothing national export earnings or the domestic effects of their instability.

National policies

What can be done purely at the *national* level to reduce export instability or the domestic impact thereof? First of all, appropriate changes in, or diversification of, the export base can reduce overall instability. Wherever possible, this should be done in such a way as not to sacrifice income, but this is not always possible. Guidance as to more stable crop combinations for particular soils and climates could, one would hope, be offered with more empirical study of supply and demand variation. With overall development, too, one would expect a more flexible, diversified and stable export-producing sector and national economy to emerge. Many countries, though by no means all, have gradually been acquiring a more diversified export commodity 'portfolio' over time (see Table 13). In particular, the development of processing facilities and further forward linkages are likely to make for a more stable export bill, although this has not been empirically verified and the example of Puerto Rico suggests the reverse (Brainard and

Cooper, 1968; Baer, 1962). To the extent that a vertically integrated industry catering in part to domestic demand emerges, export volume may become less stable while total income becomes more so.

Table 13 **Export concentration (Gini–Hirschman)**
coefficients for selected developing countries, 1954 and 1966[1]

	1954	*1966*
Ghana	0·835	0·677
Colombia	0·840	0·664
Burma	0·744	0·627
UAR	0·842	0·568
Brazil	0·612	0·471
Thailand	0·683	0·372
Tanganyika	0·446	0·358

1. The Gini-Hirschman coefficient is defined in this context as

$$\sqrt{\sum_i \left(\frac{X_i}{X_T}\right)^2}$$

where X_i is the value of exports in SITC (3 digit) category i, and X_T is total exports.

Sources: Massell (1964, p. 53).

UN (1966), *Yearbook of International Trade Statistics*, Washington.

Once all has been done that can be done with the basic instability of exports, given the willingness to trade off possible income losses for greater short-term stability, the only remaining means of reducing its domestic impact is through government action, either through 'built-in stabilizers' in the tax, pricing or welfare system, or through discretionary action. Stabilization of the economy or important sectors thereof while exports remain unstable requires the holding of greater foreign exchange, or possibly commodity, reserves, or their more efficient management through international reserve pools. The annual cost, at the margin, of this policy is the difference between the rate of return earnable through the expenditure of the extra reserves upon imports – presumably for development-orientated purposes – and that actually earned on the reserves, multiplied by that extra value of reserves which is considered just sufficient to meet the domestic stability objective. The low level of reserves held by most poor countries suggests an unwillingness to trade off very much development for the sake of stability (see Table 14).

Table 14 **Imports and foreign exchange reserves of selected developing countries, 1969** ($ US millions)

	Annual imports 1969	Foreign exchange reserves (year-end 1969)	Reserves/Imports
Argentina	1576	285	0·18
Brazil	2265	599	0·26
Mexico	2080	381	0·18
India	2028	682	0·34
Pakistan	1006	270	0·27
Philippines	1265	76	0·06
Taiwan	1205	361	0·30
Nigeria	691	107	0·15
Kenya	334	166	0·50

Source: IMF, *International Financial Statistics.*

It should be apparent that a nation is faced with policy choices with respect both to its composition of exports – and, more broadly, of its entire output – and to its allocation of wealth as between foreign exchange reserves and productive fixed capital, which is analogous to the problem of portfolio choice under uncertainty. One can conceive of an opportunity locus which indicates the possible trade-off, available through various bundles of output or various levels of foreign exchange reserves, between instability or risk and return. A policy-maker's indifference map showing willingness to trade off instability against return can then, in principle, be introduced to produce an optimum solution.

International policies
Commodity schemes (see chapter 3)

At the international level, commodity stabilization schemes invariably are directed at the level of world commodity prices rather than at volume or total earnings objectives. As long as shifts in total world demand are a source of instability in a nation's export prices – whether they are the result of shifts in total demand or in the supply from the rest of the world – international commodity price stabilization will tend to stabilize an individual producer's export earnings. Where, however, an exporter is important enough in the relevant world commodity market for fluctuations in its own supplies to exert an influence on the world price, the stabilization of that world price will reduce the damping effect, assuming the inelasticity of demand is not extreme, of price changes of the latter type on its export earnings and thereby may destabilize these earnings; whether it destabilizes or not will depend upon the relative importance of world demand fluctuations and domestic volume fluctuations. Brazil's coffee, Ghana's cocoa and Pakistan's jute are frequently cited as examples in which the stabilization of world prices might destabilize national export earnings. Note that *total* world export revenues from a particular commodity may be destabilized by a world price stabilization scheme, when price changes are primarily supply-induced, as in the case of many agricultural commodities, yet the *national* export earnings of most or all of the individual producers are likely nevertheless to be stabilized.

The devices available for international *stabilization* of world commodity prices are: (1) international long-term contracts specifying a limited range of prices in advance; (2) international agreements providing for national export quotas to regularize supplies and/or for appropriate alteration of quotas through further agreement or in a pre-stipulated manner, with variations in the world price level; (3) an international buffer stock and/or fund.

The first two are straightforward enough in principle but are subject to the difficulties discussed earlier (see chapter 3) with respect to the achievement of international agreement and effective discipline. The buffer stock or fund is an interesting special case which has been much discussed but little tried. It is a scheme providing for market intervention by an international manager of the stock-fund, who operates as an agent of the members, purchasing stocks of the commodity to support the world price when it falls to the low end of a stipulated range and selling the stocks to place a ceiling on it at the high end. The manager may also engage in the market when the price is between the two 'guaranteed' bounds to smooth undesirable fluctuations. The range may also be varied from time to time so that it becomes a 'crawling' rather than a fixed peg. A buffer stock scheme does not require full membership of producing and consuming countries in the way that a supply restriction scheme does since it works through the market. On the other hand, it requires skilled management, the tying-up of considerable capital in the fund or stock, and storage costs. It can only be applied to commodities, moreover, for which quality is fairly homogeneous and deterioration in storage can be prevented at reasonable cost.

A major stumbling block to the implementation of such schemes has been the financing of the fund-stock which must be of considerable value if it is to function effectively, that is, to hold prices within a fairly narrow range. Potential member countries have typically been unwilling to pay very large 'insurance premia' for the price stability they would thereby acquire and/or have disagreed over the distribution of this burden. The International Monetary Fund has declared its willingness, however, to provide short-term finance to its members in order to facilitate their participation in international buffer stocks under 'economically feasible' international commodity agreements, and the World Bank group is ostensibly prepared to assist in the construction and administration of such agreements. The other major difficulty with these schemes is that of arriving at international agreement on the appropriate price range and the periodic changes therein.

The only functioning buffer stock in recent years has been that of the international tin agreement which has frequently been unable to hold either its price ceiling or its price floor because of insufficient resources in the face of persistent market pressures. Releases from US stockpiles of 'strategic' commodities, including tin, while hardly international, may at times have served somewhat to stabilize specific world commodity prices as well.

Financing schemes

In addition to the schemes for stabilizing particular commodity markets, there exist international mechanisms for stabilizing individual developing countries' access to foreign exchange. These are considerably easier to construct, and both easier and more efficient to operate than commodity agreements.

The International Monetary Fund can lend to its members for the purpose of overcoming temporary balance-of-payments difficulties such as could arise from a temporary shortfall in export proceeds. First, the IMF lending can take place through its normal lending facility and in accordance with the usual practice that the first 25 per cent of a country's quota can be drawn virtually automatically, and the next 25 per cent with very few questions asked; only with further loans may the borrowing country be requested to pursue particular IMF-approved policies to bring its balance of payments into equilibrium. The IMF has lent considerable sums under this facility in the past. Since the interest rate on these loans is relatively low and the foreign exchange thus made available is untied with respect to either projects or to procurement, these balance-of-payments loans have constituted an important flow of 'foreign aid' to developing countries, though usually unrecorded as such. As of March 1971, IMF loans to developing countries of this regular type, beyond their original subscriptions, stood at $736 millions (IMF).

In recognition of the peculiarly difficult problems of the poor primary-exporting members of the IMF, the Fund introduced a special 'compensatory financing' scheme a few years ago to make it possible for these countries to gain automatic access to further IMF loans when their exports fell below the current trend, defined as a five-year moving average centred on the current shortfall year. Subsequently eased, the terms of this facility at present grant primary-exporting countries access to up to 50 per cent of their IMF quota, in addition to their conventional borrowing rights under the terms of the IMF agreement. The amounts made available under the terms of the compensatory financing facility have so far been relatively modest.

This facility offers assistance for short-term export instability. It does not, however, provide for cases in which the exports of a particular country are facing a steady and unexpected downward movement. If, for instance, the price projected for a country's major export over a five-year planning period turns out to have been much too high, there is no facility for assisting the country in question to overcome the balance-of-payments difficulties which will inevitably result. For this purpose another facility has been suggested – the so-called 'supplementary finance' scheme. Supplementary financing is suggested for cases where the export performance falls below reasonable prior expectations, as agreed upon by the lending agency and prospective borrowers in advance. This facility has yet to be brought into operation but it is an obvious further international device for assisting countries to overcome slightly longer-term problems of export instability.

Special drawing rights in the International Monetary Fund are also available to all IMF members to assist them to overcome balance-of-payments difficulties. These consist of allocations of internationally acceptable purchasing power, created by mutual agreement in order to assure an adequate supply of world liquidity. Whereas the occasion of their creation provided an opportunity for substantially increasing the foreign exchange availability of the poorest members of the world community, this opportunity was not seized. Arguing that the two issues of world liquidity and foreign aid should not be confused by addressing them both with the same policy instrument, the IMF's key members voted to assign the special drawing rights to the IMF members in accordance with their quota and voting rights. This procedure accorded the developed industrial countries 69 per cent of the total SDR allocation of $9·5 billion over the first three years. The possibility of linking SDR creation with foreign assistance in the future is at present under review.

6 Import Substitution

Disillusion with export prospects, the desire for rapid growth and for industrialization, and the pressure of balance-of-payments difficulties have pushed the strategy of import substitution to the fore in many developing countries during the past two decades. Import substitution may be undertaken not only with respect to manufactured products, which are usually the main focus for discussions of this strategy, but also with respect to primary products, particularly food, and services, such as banking, insurance and international transport. The same considerations apply to the economic analysis of each. Since the discussion usually is concerned with manufactures, that is the context in which this discussion of import substitution will also be placed.

Measurement of import substitution

What exactly is meant by the term 'import substitution', and how can one measure its achievement? There obviously exist different possible ways of defining it but the usual present convention is as follows. Import substitution is said to have occurred when the *proportion* of total supply of a particular commodity or group of commodities which is obtained through imports rather than through domestic production has declined in the country concerned. Any change in a country's imports between time period t_0 and time period t_1 can be decomposed into that element which is attributable to a change in the total supply, or demand, of the commodity or commodities in question (which is itself primarily a function of national income), and that element which is the product of import substitution. Thus,

$$M_1 - M_0 = m_1 S_1 - m_0 S_0$$
$$= S_1 (m_1 - m_0) + m_0 (S_1 - S_0)$$

where M_t is imports, S_t is total supply (domestic production plus imports), m is M_t/S_t, and the subscripts refer to the time periods being compared. If some of the domestic production is sold for export, S_t may be further decomposed into home consumption and exports.

The first term in the above equation $[S_1 (m_1 - m_0)]$ is an absolute measure of gross import substitution. It is gross because it relates to the final product regardless of the possibility of imported intermediate inputs and/or factor services. If one wants to compare the extent of import substitution as between industries, time periods or countries, one may prefer to have relative measures, in which case the absolute measure can be divided by the change in domestic output. That is, relative gross import substitution is

$$\frac{S_1 (m_1 - m_0),}{Q_t - Q_0}$$

where Q_t is domestic output in period t and

$$Q_1 - Q_0 = S_1 (1 - m_1) - S_0 (1 - m_0).$$

Alternatively, one could employ, for this purpose, the proportionate change in the import ratio. That is, $\frac{m_1 - m_0}{m_0}$.

A better, but more difficult, measure of import substitution would measure the extent to which value added by nationally owned factors, measured at world prices, has replaced value added by non-national factors in the productive activity in question. The S_t's and Q_t's in the above expressions would then refer to productive processes or activities rather than to final products.

At what level of aggregation can one usefully measure import substitution in this manner? It does not make much sense to consider import substitution at the level of the entire economy, for then it would simply measure changes in the degree of 'openness', or even at that of the total industrial sector, for this still conceals too much. Probably most fruitful is the concept's application to major components of the industrial sector – such as capital goods, consumer goods, intermediate inputs – and to individual industries or processes.

The other side of the import substitution coin is the concomitant alteration in the structure of imports. To the extent that substitution takes place in the form of domestic production for what was formerly imported, the total import bill will be reduced or the foreign exchange thereby freed will be employed for the import of something else. In either case, the composition of the total import bill will be altered. Industrial import-substitution typically leads to an increase in the share of intermediate inputs, such as fuel, spare parts, components, etc., in the import bill. In the case of most developing countries the import substitution which has taken place has also led to a shift from consumer-goods to capital-goods in the import bill.

Differing backgrounds for import substitution

The motivation for import substitution has varied from place to place and from period to period. It has not always been part of a government's conscious development strategy as much of the critical literature seems to suggest. Some import substitution is the product of the 'natural' growth process; as the domestic market grows with economic development, one would expect that more domestic industries would emerge spontaneously to supply it, with or without governmental support. Import substitution in these circumstances reduces the cost to the economy of acquiring the goods or services in question.

Import substitution which occurs in response to the growth of domestic markets presumably gradually moves from industries which benefit from few scale economies towards industries which require a progressively larger and larger minimum scale. Small countries will fairly quickly exhaust the possibilities for such 'natural' import substitution in domestic markets; weak domestic transport systems also frequently create great difficulty and convert ostensibly large countries into economically small ones in which potential scale economies can still not be realized. A considerable 'backlog' of previously unexploited import substitution possibilities has existed until recently in many developing countries. It is worth asking why this type of import substitution did not occur sooner in many parts of the Third World in which the market size would clearly have made domestic manufacturing production for the local market possible. The answer lies in the incentive structure within the underdeveloped areas which, at least in the colonies, was itself the product of pressures from producers in the metropolitan countries, the major trading firms and/or local export-producing interests, none of whom stood to benefit from a diminution of traditional import trade.

Work by Chenery and others has offered suggestive insights into the 'normal' pattern of demand for and supply of industrial products as population and per capita income expand. Cross-sectional analysis of fourteen major categories of manufacturing in thirty-eight countries in the early 1950s indicated that, on average, import substitution, as defined above, accounted for 50 per cent of industrial expansion between the income levels of $100 and $600 per capita. While there was considerable uniformity of experience in the 'growth elasticity' of various types of industrial *supply*, or demand, there was much greater variation in the 'growth elasticity' of different types of industrial *production*. Individual countries tend to have industrial sectors which reflect their size, level of per capita income and resource base (Chenery, 1960; Chenery and Taylor, 1968). Other work indicates that the 'normal' extent of import substituting industrial growth has been much greater in the newly-industrializing states in the twentieth century than it was in the older industrial states, both in the same (twentieth century) period and in that earlier period during which the latter had per capita incomes of the same levels as the 'new' industrializers (Maizels, 1963).

Import substitution has also been the product of economic necessity in periods when normal international trading relationships were interrupted. The Great Depression of the 1930s and the Second World War severely disrupted the normal channels of trade and created 'abnormally' attractive opportunities for domestic manufacturing production *vis-à-vis* the suppliers of manufactured goods from the rest of the world. It also created incentives for other non-industrial import substitution activities. In many Latin American countries these disruptions significantly influenced the speed and pattern of industrial growth. Since supplies of key intermediate industrial inputs were also interrupted by the war, the fillip it offered to indigenous industry was not general, but a highly selective one. The trauma of the Depression not only had short-term effects, but also deeply affected the conceptions of politicians and planners, particularly in Latin America, as to the most appropriate national economic strategies thereafter.

Many developing countries have drifted into more and more import-substituting activities in response to balance-of-payments pressures, which are themselves the product of the rapidly rising import demand implicit in an accelerated development programme and insufficiently rapid export growth. Most countries are unwilling to be constrained to the rate of growth of the bottleneck sector, which may frequently be the one engaged in the sale of 'traditional exports'. Import substitution policies often seemed easier to implement than export promotion ones, given the weak state of world markets for the exports they happened to have.

Trade barriers were usually, in any case, imposed at an early stage upon luxury-goods in order to preserve scarce foreign exchange for other higher priority uses; the unintentional outcome was the growth of domestic luxury-good industries, sometimes highly import-intensive and foreign-owned, in response to the profit opportunities the trade barriers created. Some argue that most developing countries inevitably end up facing severe balance-of-payments pressures which tend to 'close' their economies; but 'closing' and import substitution may not be the only response to these pressures and cannot, in any case, be continuing ones. Where countries have 'drifted' into import substitution in this way, one must ask what the balance-of-payments impact has been and, to the extent that it has been favourable, at what overall resource cost it has been purchased. Industrial import substitution can also be and has frequently been pursued as a matter of conscious national developmental strategy for the sake of industrialization itself, foreign exchange conservation, employment creation, long-term income maximization or all of these simultaneously. It can also be part of a policy of economic nationalism which can be interpreted as an attempt by decision-makers not to *raise* national income so much as to redistribute it. Such a redistribution is likely to be in their own interest in that it would particularly favour urban dwellers and the more skilled and educated classes – and increase the potential for state control – since those who, in fact, carried the real burden of such redistribution were not so much the foreigners as domestic rural dwellers and the unemployed.

Import substitution in practice

Since the lack of a coherent strategy is also implicitly a 'strategy', it makes some sense to view *all* import substitution *experience*, whether planned or not, in terms of what might have been obtainable had an optimal set of policies been pursued. The sad conclusion most commentators have reached is that, whatever the merits of industrial import substitution as a policy target – and most would accept it, within reasonable limits, as a quite legitimate one – it has been implemented rather badly.

Import substitution has typically begun with manufactured consumer-goods for which there was already an obvious local market. There may be danger, incidentally, in over-reliance on import data for gauging whether an adequate local market exists to justify domestic production of a particular commodity. In the first place, trade data are not typically disaggregated to the degree necessary and can, especially for consumer goods, conceal considerable product differentiation under even an apparently fairly narrowly defined category. Secondly, if tariff protection is required for the good in question, one must be prepared to experience some consequent reduction in the market as a result of the existence of demand elasticity. Many consumer goods can be produced efficiently at relatively small scale and/or are labour-intensive in their production. Comparative advantage has typically been helped along by tariff and other protective structures which are normally biased against the domestic production of capital goods or intermediate industrial inputs and in favour of consumer goods (see chapter 8). During this early stage of import substitution, it is relatively easy to achieve rapid rates of industrial growth and, if foreign exchange saving occurs, to expand the economy at a rate greater than export growth alone would have permitted.

Table 15 **Imports as a percentage of total supplies, selected developing countries, 1948–65**[1]

	Consumer goods %	Intermediate goods %	Capital goods %
Pakistan			
1951/2	77·5	73·2	76·3
1964/5	11·4	15·0	62·3
Philippines			
1948	30·9	90·3	79·7
1965	4·7	36·3	62·9
Brazil			
1949	9·0	25·9	63·7
1964	1·3	6·6	9·8
India			
1951	4·2	17·4	56·5
1961	1·4	18·7	42·4
Mexico			
1950	2·4	13·2	66·5
1960	1·3	10·4	54·9

1. These data are not strictly comparable. See original source for details.
Source: Little, Scitovsky and Scott (1970, p. 60).

Tables 15 and 16 show the progress in import substitution in a selected few countries, and the resulting alterations in the structure of imports. It is clear from Table 15 that the percentage of total supplies met by imports is far greater for capital goods than it is for consumer goods. Only Brazil has achieved a substantial measure of autonomy with respect to its supplies of capital goods. The import substitution which occurred in the 1950s and early 1960s in Pakistan and the Philippines was clearly most heavily oriented towards consumer goods. From Table 16, it can be seen that the impact of these import substitution efforts upon the import bill has been to shift away from consumer goods imports and towards intermediate and capital goods imports. The relatively high share of consumer goods in the Nigerian and Tanzanian import bills is typical of the African scene and reflects the relatively underdeveloped character of African industrialization.

Two outcomes of the import substitution process were unforeseen and have proven troublesome. The first is the failure of the process to free the economy from dependence on the world economy. Much of the import substitution which has taken place has been undertaken by foreign investors, usually intent on defending their export markets against domestic or other foreign competition. Their interest, profits, royalties and management fees constitute relatively fixed claims upon the balance-of-payments which, together with imported intermediate inputs, must be set against the gross value of import substitution. Indeed, the post-import-substitution economy is typically *more* vulnerable to fluctuations in external receipts than the 'traditional' export economy was, in that its import bill has been trimmed to 'essentials' – intermediate inputs for its new industrial sector, capital goods required for its development programme, and essential food (see Table 16). There is no longer any import 'fat' available to absorb export fluctuations at least in part.

The second outcome is the tendency of the import-substitution process to 'get stuck' without generating any linkage effects of the type to which Hirschman (1968) directed so much attention. Inefficient import substitution, far from generating further industrialization, may actually inhibit the development process by increasing the costs of inputs to potentially forward-linked industries. Moreover, those first into the industrial sector may oppose the development of backward-linked industrial suppliers for fear they will be less efficient and reliable suppliers than the existing world market sources. There may thus arise both market and political blockages to the further development of manufacturing industry after the easy first stage of import substitution has been completed. To some extent these may be overcome where one firm or the state is the relevant actor in the linkage development.

Table 16 **Structure of imports, selected developing countries, 1877–1969**

	Consumer goods %	Intermediate goods %	Capital goods %	Total
Brazil				
1948–50	15	47[1]	38	100
1960–62	9	62[1]	29	100
Nigeria				
1950	60	10	30	100
1965	45	24	31	100
Mexico				
1877–78	75	15	10	100
1910–11	43	27	30	100
1940	28	44	28	100
1960	11	45	44	100
Argentina				
1900–04	42[3]	37	21	100
1910–14	37	33	30	100
1925–29	37	31	32	100
1960–63	5	62	33	100
Tanzania				
1962	51[2]	14	35	100
1969	33[2]	21	46	100

1. Includes wheat: 6 per cent in 1948–50, 13 per cent in 1960–62.
2. Includes miscellaneous: 3 per cent in 1962, 2 per cent in 1969.
3. Includes miscellaneous: 3 per cent.

Sources: Bergsman (1970, p. 16).
Diaz Alejandro (1970, pp. 15, 517).
Kilby (1969, p. 27).
King (1970, pp. 6, 21).
United Republic of Tanzania (1970, p. 4).

The most frequent pattern has been for the import-substituting industrialization process to 'get stuck' on the threshold of development of intermediate and capital goods industries. Nor in these circumstances is there much hope for developing manufactured exports. The usually observed sequence of consumer goods to capital goods production reflects governmental policies and perceptions as much as the necessary economics of manufacturing production. There have arisen efficient capital goods industries in many countries without any protection or incentives whatsoever. Increasing attention is now necessarily being devoted to these cases as the opportunities for successful consumer-good import substitution are filled up. It is clear that capital goods industries in developing countries may themselves be labour-intensive and need not depend upon scale economies; particularly is this so in the case of 'custom-made' machinery. While the skill-intensity of these industries may still be high, some have evidently prospered, at least in Latin America and South Asia, despite it (Baer, 1969; Leff, 1968; Bergsman, 1970).

Further advantages are sometimes seen in emphasizing capital goods import substitution at the expense of other types. In a closed economy without the opportunity for international trade, capital goods must be produced if the savings of an economy are to be translated into investment. Capital goods production in this case determines the level of investment. This has led some with autarchic leanings or lack of confidence in the foreign exchange earning capabilities of their economies to advocate the building of domestic capital goods industries as a matter of the very highest priority. A model based upon either autarchic objectives or stagnant demand for the export products which it could produce with its relatively rigid production structure, lay behind the Second Indian Five-Year Plan's heavy emphasis upon capital goods production. A more sophisticated rationale for emphasizing capital goods import substitution is that only the development of indigenous capital goods production can halt the continuing practice of importing inappropriate technologies into the developing countries. Rising wage rates in the industrial countries guarantee that machinery and equipment will become ever more capital-intensive; the innovations which are introduced are all likely to be labour-saving rather than capital-saving. Thus the creation of local capital goods industries are likely to increase the poor countries' degree of control over the direction and spread of technical change. It might be added that a wider conception of capital goods would include educational and research facilities and personnel, in which the need for appropriate locally oriented changes in technology is at least as great as in manufacturing industry.

All things considered, it is difficult to find any rationale for the pattern of import substituting industrialization which has, whether consciously or not, actually been promoted. It has given undue emphasis to consumer goods in most countries; it has given insufficient attention to potential long-run comparative advantages, i.e. resource endowments and learning possibilities; and it has employed alien and unsuitable, i.e. capital-intensive technologies to an extraordinary and unnecessary degree. If a selective approach to import substitution is to be pursued at all, and there is a strong case to be made for a more generalized approach, the selection actually employed in recent years has left a great deal to be desired. The consequence has too frequently been the creation of an inefficient industrial sector operating far below capacity, and creating very little employment, very little foreign exchange saving, and little prospect of further productivity growth. The object of policy must now be gradually to bring incentive structures and thus the relative efficiencies of various industrial activities into some sort of balance, thereby encouraging domestic manufacture of intermediate and capital goods at the expense of importable consumer goods and the development eventually of manufacture for export.

7 Commercial Policy

It should by now be clear that government commercial policy and exchange rate policy are important potential instruments for the implementation of national development policy which can have a variety of strategic objectives of its own. These policies can only be evaluated in the context of the specific objectives set for itself by the country in question. General policy prescriptions, *in vacuo*, such as 'free trade' or 'industrial protection' do not usually make a great deal of sense to the policymaker in a specific national context.

Commercial policy in context

There are many instruments other than commercial and exchange rate policy which can also be employed for industrial promotion, export diversification, employment creation, or the pursuit of whatever other development-oriented strategies are being pushed. Tax relief, direct subsidies, provision of infrastructure and cheap credit are among the alternative possibilities. In order properly to evaluate a development programme's impact one has to consider the complete package of incentives and disincentives, both planned and unplanned.

Economists have long inveighed against the use of tariffs and other trade barriers as protective devices on the grounds that they are inefficient policy instruments relative to other alternatives which create the same effects. If, for instance, the intention is to stimulate a particular industry, it makes more sense to offer a direct subsidy to that industry than to impose a protective tariff or other import restriction, since it avoids the price increase and both the resulting distortion of consumption and the inappropriate apportionment of the 'tax' burden which a trade barrier carries with it. A subsidy is also more likely to be subjected to periodic review. If it is possible to identify those activities within the industry or productive enterprise which are considered worthy of support – presumably because of the external benefits they throw off, such as training or research or employment – it would be better still to offer direct subsidies only to those activities rather than to the firm or industry as a whole. Still, import and export tariffs, other trade barriers and exchange rate policies have been of prime policy importance in most developing countries where there is still heavy reliance upon market forces for the management of their economies. In developing countries, to the many other forces which produce tariffs instead of subsidies in all countries is added the over-whelming problem of scarce government revenues. In part, the incentive structures which have been their result have been quite unintended and imperfectly understood. In part, the policies pursued have been quite consciously selected as preferable to the available alternative policy mixes.

Partial analysis of tariffs and quotas

If a country chooses to employ commercial policy in order to pursue objectives relating to the structure of production and development, rather than merely as a matter of raising government revenues, or reducing short-run demand or balance-of-payments pressures, it will wish to choose between tariffs and physical controls. In the context of developing countries, where skilled and efficient administration is in short supply, the balance of advantage will almost always rest with tariffs. The administration of tariff collection is everywhere well established and relatively simple. Controls and licensing schemes are, by their very nature, much more complicated to administer and therefore more likely to lead to delays, inefficiencies and corruption. Quotas are also less predictable in their economic impact – although more so in their degree of physical restriction – in that the extent of the protection they offer is a function of the total level of demand. When demand is increasing for the commodity in question, a physical control which begins by merely restricting imports to the same extent as an import tariff will become considerably more protective over time. Physical controls are likely to be superior to tariffs only in those cases where the object of policy is to prohibit totally the importation of some good or service.

Figure 4 uses the tools of traditional partial equilibrium analysis to portray the effects of tariffs and quotas upon the production and consumption of a specific good. In most cases, the world price of the importable is more or less given to the individual country in question, as is shown by the infinitely elastic world supply curve WW', at price OW. A tariff imposed at the rate TW/OW will raise the domestic price to OT, thereby inducing domestic producers, whose supply curve is WSS', to expand their production, quite possibly nonexistent before, to OQ and, with the domestic demand curve shown by DD', reducing domestic consumption from OC to OE. The government collects revenues of $TW.QE$, or the area of the rectangle $GHJK$, from its tariff. Government could have generated the identical consumption and production effects, although it would have lost its revenues to private importers and/or foreign producers, had it imposed a physical import quota in the amount of QE ($=GH$). If, however, in a subsequent period, demand rose from DD' to DD'', the effects of the tariff and quota would diverge. In the case of the tariff, the domestic price would remain unchanged and the extra demand would be supplied by the world market unless domestic producers had increased their productivity in the meantime. In the case of the quota of $GH(=MN)$, however, the domestic price would have to increase to OP, and the extra demand, EF, would be wholly supplied by domestic producers ($EF=QR$), who now receive more protection from competitive imports than they did before and more than is offered by the import tariff.

If the supply curve in this diagram accurately portrays the social rather than merely the private costs of producing the goods in question, the area under the supply curve (WSG) less the costs of acquiring on the world market the supplies now locally produced ($OQ.OW$) portrays the unnecessary short-run cost to the economy of producing at a higher cost than the rest of the world under the protection of tariffs or quotas. This cost is given, then, by the area SGK. Similarly, there is an unnecessary

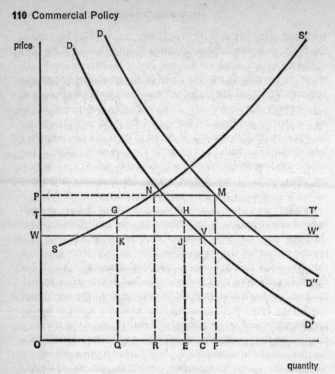

Figure 4

loss of consumers' surplus produced by the increase in the domestic price; this is shown by the difference between the area under the demand curve but over the world price under free trade when, with demand curve DD', consumption was OC at price OW, and the corresponding area under protection when consumption was OE at price OT. That is, $DVW - DHJW = HVJ$. Whether these costs are worth incurring depends upon the motivation for having imposed the trade barriers in the first place.

Arguments for tariffs and protection

There is a vast literature concerning the use of the tariff. Discussion of the various arguments for the use of tariffs and trade barriers obviously incorporates consideration of some of the broader aspects of development strategy which have been discussed earlier. General arguments for the use of tariffs and trade barriers, except in the cases of the government revenue and terms of trade arguments, come down to arguments as to the appropriate degree of openness for an economy. Arguments usually put forward for industrial tariff protection also have less to do with the use of the tariff or trade barrier policy instrument than with the rationale for industrialization. The arguments for greater selectivity in the application of protection are also typically arguments about development objectives rather than about the use of particular policy instruments.

Ideally, one ought to argue through the national developmental objectives and intermediate targets, and then consider this particular set of policy instruments, among others, available for the pursuit of the stated objectives. If only because of the way in which this material is conventionally segmented for discussion elsewhere, however, it makes some sense to run through the most common arguments here. In the context of developing countries it is worth distinguishing between (a) the arguments which are *general* arguments for trade barriers or tariffs, (b) those which are *general* arguments for *industrial* protection, and (c) those which are intended to provide criteria for the *selection* of activities for protection. Those which are most worth discussing in this context may be summarized as:

1. General arguments for tariffs:
   (a) the government revenue argument;
   (b) the balance-of-payments argument;
   (c) the terms of trade argument;
   (d) the risk aversion argument.
2. General arguments for industrial protection:
   (a) the general 'infant economy' argument for industrial protection;
   (b) the second-best argument based upon labour market imperfections;
   (c) the external economies argument.
3. Arguments for selective protection

(a) the infant industry argument;
(b) the terms of trade argument specific to a particular productive activity;
(c) the external economy argument applied to a particular productive activity;
(d) the risk aversion argument applied to a particular productive activity.

General arguments for tariffs and protection

In circumstances in which accounting skills are scarce both in the private and the state sector, where administrative competence and incorruptibility is imperfect, and record-keeping rare, it is extremely difficult to raise government revenues through such devices as income and property taxes. One of the easiest and cheapest devices for collecting taxes in poor countries is to levy them on produce which is passing in or out of the country and which therefore normally has to be funnelled through a relatively few ports or border posts at which administrative control is feasible. It should not therefore be surprising that foreign trade taxes constitute the major source of government revenues in most developing countries. In fact the share of total government revenues in GNP in poor countries has been found to be correlated not with GNP itself or with ideological complexion but rather with the degree of openness, i.e. the share of imports and exports in GNP, these being the activities most easily taxable (Hinrichs, 1965). In that virtually all governments of poor countries aspire to a large role in the development of their economies, taxes upon foreign trade are an inevitable part of the fiscal system. Analyses which recommend the abolition of import tariffs and their replacement by direct government subsidies not only have to explain where the revenue for the subsidies is to come from but also where revenue to replace that lost by the duty abolition will be found. Governments seeking to promote import-substituting industries are likely also for the same reason to prefer high import tariffs over a devalued currency, other things being equal, although success with the policy will eliminate the imports which constitute the base for the tax. Given the need for government revenue, then, particularly at the lowest levels of income, one must put up with a certain degree of 'inward orientation' as a result of foreign trade taxes, whatever one's view of the desirability of 'openness'. (One could also construct a related case for governments' maintenance or creation not only of tariffs but also of import controls, which need not create government revenues, based upon civil servants' self-interest in maximizing their own employment and/or other gains.) In the absence of other arguments one might, from the revenue argument alone, expect a uniform *ad valorem* tariff on all imports with perhaps extra duties on luxury-goods for the sake of progressiveness, and a (perhaps different) uniform *ad valorem* tax on all exports.

Balance-of-payments pressures arising from accelerated development programmes, and insufficiently rapidly rising export proceeds, are frequently cited as another major ground for the erection of import tariffs and other trade barriers. Studies of many countries imply that there are certain imported inputs which are essential for growth and which cannot be produced in the short run at home, and that the growth rate is therefore constrained by the rate of growth in export revenues with which these imports may be purchased. Export growth rates are very frequently insufficient for the attainment of the local planners' growth targets; nor are foreign capital inflows usually large enough to offset these shortfalls. Balance-of-payments crises then emerge from fruitless attempts to proceed with the planned programmes. Others see the inevitability of a more rapid rate of growth in import demand than in GNP as a consequence of changing demand patterns with per capita income growth, urbanization and improved international communications. Whatever the precise cause, there may well be growing balance-of-payments problems with accelerated development, which will create pressures towards 'closing' the economy, pressures which are exceedingly difficult to resist. As this occurs, the government has more than one policy weapon to bring to bear upon the problem. The import tariff, import quotas, exchange controls, and a variety of encouragements to exports, can all be employed. Again, in the absence of arguments for selectivity, the most plausible being that of distributional equity, the presumption is that these measures will be employed so as to conserve and earn foreign exchange uniformly in all types of economic activity. (A much simpler device for achieving the same objective may be devaluation, about which more later.)

There are at least two other arguments for turning the economy generally 'inward', despite the basic logic of comparative advantage, which moreover are not necessarily arguments for specifically industrial protection. The first is the argument which states that in certain circumstances – those where the nation has market power either in import or in export markets – trade restriction can improve the terms of trade. Developing countries are such small actors in world markets, however, that each one is certainly a price-taker as far as its imports are concerned. (There may still be some limited room for manoeuvre with respect to which products and prices to take.) While single developing countries may face declining world demand curves for individual export commodities (as was seen in chapter 2), none could expect to have market power in more than a very few; it follows that improvements in the terms of trade through trade restriction are best pursued on a commodity-specific basis with respect to particular exports through export duties, Marketing Board trading surpluses and other such devices, rather than through an overall policy of trade restriction.

The second argument posits that individual countries may rationally seek to reduce their risks, even if it involves them in some continuing costs, by supplying themselves to a greater extent with at least some of their key inputs, such as food. Self-sufficiency may involve the use of resources which would be more efficiently employed, on a strict cost-benefit basis, in production for exports, the revenues from which could then, in a certain world, be spent upon the importation of the inputs in question. Risk aversion on the part of governments of poor nations should not surprise anyone.

General arguments for industrial protection

Industrialization, as we have seen, has been regarded as a major contributing element in the development process by many

writers and by even more governments. Trade barriers constitute one instrument for its stimulation; exchange rate policies
are another. Presumably, if the import tariff is to be employed
to this end it should be a uniform tariff against all industrial
imports; this would not, however, create uniform levels of
effective protection for all import-competing manufacturing
industries (see chapter 8). Nor would it offer equivalent encouragement to exporting manufacturing industries, for while
they, like everyone else, would enjoy (presumably unnecessary)
protection in home markets, they would be selling upon world
markets in which they receive no such incentives. An *ad
valorem* subsidy to manufactured exports of the same size as
the uniform industrial import duty would help to set this right
but has obvious fiscal implications and is formally in contra-
vention of the GATT. (The fiscal problem would probably be
insignificant in most developing countries at present because of
their limited success with manufactured exports.) Devaluation
by the same percentage as the import duty would be a simple
and effective alternative, but it would, of course, not discriminate between industry and non-industry, which was, in
this case, the purpose of the protection programme.

There exist other arguments for general industrial protection
based upon the existence of market imperfections. Industrial
wage rates exceed rural wage rates, it has been argued, and this
creates a disincentive to manufacturing relative to agriculture.
Without raising the question as to whether this is always the
case, or whether it may be compensated for by offsetting price
distortions in the capital market, it should be clear that this
phenomenon does not constitute an argument for industrial
protection but, rather, is an argument for rectifying the distortion in the labour market with an employment subsidy to all
the sectors affected by it, some of which may not be industrial.

An analogous response in terms of subsidies is appropriate
to the claim that 'industry' generates external economies for
which it should be rewarded, or the argument that calls for
tariff protection in order to create industrial jobs. If the
government revenue constraint makes the subsidies, which are
preferable, difficult or impossible, tariff and exchange rate

measures can, of course, be employed as second-best policy instruments – at which point one must return to the argument in the preceding paragraph.

Arguments for selective protection

When one looks at the tariff schedule or the structure of incentives, however measured, in developing or any other countries, one does not see uniform treatment of all activities. It is time now to look at the criteria for selectivity in the application of tariffs, trade barriers and other incentives to domestic production. Selectivity refers to deviation from the 'normal' degree of incentive offered either to any form of domestic production or, if the chosen strategy is to promote industry, to any industrial activity. Thus if one has accepted that there exists a case for both 'closing' the economy in general and for generalized industrial protection, one would expect, in the absence of further selectivity, to observe a uniform rate of protection for all industrial activity and another lower uniform rate of protection for all other activity – or what would amount to a dual exchange rate system (see chapter 9).

The best known and most legitimate argument for selective protection is the infant industry argument. It is based upon the presumption that those engaged in a new form of production *learn* to conduct it more efficiently over time but are not perfectly confident themselves that this learning will take place. An infant industry tariff is intended to remain in place only for as long as is necessary for the industry or firm in question to acquire the skill which will enable it to compete with producers in the rest of the world on a basis no more favoured than domestic producers of other products. There undoubtedly do exist temporary problems of moving into production, establishing marketing outlets, and so forth, in most industrial activities, which produce higher returns in later years than in earlier ones; however, whether these learning effects are such that they cannot be taken into account by the businessmen concerned is another matter. Governments may well know better, be less risk-averse, or see that private risk exceeds social risk, with respect to learning effects, and so justify the tariff on these grounds. Most 'infant industry tariffs' are actually industrial subsidy schemes, pure and simple, however, in which the subsidy is intended to be concentrated during a particular period in the life of the industry. Unfortunately, these intentions are frequently not realized and the special treatment is difficult to remove. In principle, this argument offers justification for selectivity in industrial protection – the point being to encourage only those industries with potential learning effects – rather than acting as a catch-all rationalization for early-stage industrial subsidies, which unfortunately is how it is frequently employed.

Many import and export duties were, and in some cases still are, introduced primarily for their revenue effects. Vertical – distributional – equity has weighed heavily in the selection of items to carry the heaviest revenue tariffs. Luxury consumer-goods have traditionally borne the heaviest import taxes, and particularly profitable export production the heaviest export duties. If selective import duties or other controls upon non-essential imports are not offset by equivalent taxes upon domestic production (which may not, in fact, even yet exist), there will be supernormal incentives favouring the domestic production of the items in question. For this reason, among others, consumer-goods industries catering to the demands of the wealthy have frequently been among the first industries to appear in newly industrializing countries.

Similar considerations apply to the introduction of tariff and trade barriers introduced for balance-of-payments reasons. It has been common practice to cut back upon the importation of 'non-essentials' while continuing to permit capital goods and intermediate inputs to domestic industries to be imported free of any restrictions. As far as the structure of domestic incentives is concerned, this has imparted a bias against the development of local capital goods and input industries and in favour of consumer goods industries. Again, it would have been more appropriate to tax domestic production of non-essentials as well as imports in order to avoid undesirable incentive effects for domestic production. This could be achieved by replacing the import duty with a sales tax in those cases where it is a tariff rather than a direct control which is being employed.

As has been seen, the objective of self-sufficiency may also lead to some selectivity in the use of trade barriers. Certain imports may be perceived as particularly strategic and/or vulnerable – food, basic fuel, industrial inputs – and therefore prime objects for import substitution. The terms of trade argument also was seen to become an argument for selective application of export duties in the context of less-developed countries.

The selectivity issue is really nothing less than the whole issue of development strategy – which activities to encourage the most. In addition to considerations of dynamic comparative advantage, learning potential, external economies and potential terms of trade gains, one may be including locational questions, employment and other targets in the social welfare function. In the absence of *clear* criteria for selection, there is an obvious presumption that uniform treatment is best. Particular cases must be judged against the norm. The structure of incentives imparted by the present trade and exchange rate policies of the developing countries typically has biases and degrees of dispersion which do not reflect these countries' own statements of policy and, having been created by a long series of almost random marginal alterations, no longer contain any basic rationale (see chapter 8). In reaction to the policy mistakes of the past, there has recently been increased interest on the part of many governments in developing countries in 'liberalization' of their importing policies. This liberalization has had two strands to it: (1) increased openness of the entire economy; and (2) increased reliance upon indirect policy instruments and the market relative to direct controls.

This discussion has so far been couched primarily in terms of protection against imports. Commercial policy can equally be applied to the artificial stimulation of exports, either generally or, more frequently found in practice, with respect only to industrial exports. In order to offset a general import duty, as has been observed, a country ought, on efficiency grounds, at least to have a general export subsidy of the same size. While this combination of generalized import duty and export subsidy is rarely observed – since it is equivalent to currency devaluation, the preferred alternative – commercial policy *is* frequently applied to the subsidy (equals protection) of particular export activities. The structure of export duties must be analysed just as closely as that of import duties to uncover the differential incentives offered to various types of export activity. Apart from export duties, schemes for the rebate of import duties and/or domestic sales taxes, physical export controls, and differential exchange rates must also be weighed for their effects upon export development.

8 The Measurement of Protection

In order to be able to discuss commercial and exchange rate policy fruitfully, it is necessary to have tools not only for analysing but also for measuring the domestic impact of tariff and other trade restrictions. With the exception of the revenue tariff, trade barriers are imposed with the express purpose of inducing the economic actors in the country in question to behave in a manner which differs from that in which they would behave were there no barriers to free international trade; and even the revenue tariff creates incentive effects. The objective of measurement may be to ascertain the aggregative impact of a country's various trade barriers for the sake of making appropriate macro-economic policy with respect to the level of aggregate demand or the exchange rate, or for the purpose of checking the progress of longer-term strategy as to the degree of openness; alternatively, it may be to discover the impact of trade barriers at the sectoral level, or at a quite micro level upon a particular industry or firm.

Tariff averages
Attempts to measure the overall 'average height of the tariff' have been fairly frequent in the older empirical literature of international trade. The crudest and oldest method is simply to measure the value of import duties collected as a percentage of the value of total imports, or sometimes as a percentage of the value of total dutiable imports. Similar methodology can be employed to measure the average level of export duty. This measure suffers from the major disadvantage that it weights each rate of import tariff by the value of imports of the item in question and that value is itself affected by the height of the tariff; thus where demand elasticities are greater than zero

this average measure will understate the true height of the tariff. (A tariff so high that it shut out imports entirely would not enter into the calculation of the tariff average at all!) Alternative procedures for averaging which have been proposed include weighting each tariff listed in the tariff schedule equally, or weighting by total domestic consumption (domestic production plus imports), or by total consumption in other similar nations with fewer trade barriers. While such tariff measures can tell one something of the average change in trade barriers over time, there are obvious limits to their usefulness for any particular policy decision.

Tariff structure

Policy decisions more frequently relate to the imposition or removal of particular trade barriers which affect particular industries than to the aggregate of trade barriers for the entire economy. Thus it is not the overall average which is of interest to the policymaker so much as the degree and nature of the dispersion of the trade barriers. The former is of interest for the light it sheds upon the choice between home and foreign purchases and production *in general*, but the latter enable him to see what incentives are being established as between the various specific sectors and industries. Commercial policy typically has a greater impact upon the pattern of development through changes in the structure or dispersion of the tariff than through changes in its average height.

Apart from the growing realization in recent years that tariff structure is more important to the policymaker than tariff height, because of the powerful differential incentive effects which can be contained within the tariff schedule, there has been a considerable increase in the degree of sophistication of tariff measurement. On the face of it, one might address oneself to the structure (or dispersion) question by analysing the rates listed in the tariff schedule – constructing appropriate subcategories of the overall average. Some tariff data organized in this fashion are shown in Table 17. One might then use these rates together with other data to conduct empirical partial analysis of the type shown in Figure 4. In using nominal import duty data of this type, it is essential to consider them net of sales or excise duties which are levied only upon domestic production of the items in question, for such taxes act as an offset to tariffs upon imports. The difference this makes is evident in the Pakistani data in Table 17, which shows both 'gross' and 'net' average import duty rates.

Table 17 **Average rates of nominal import duty, by end use category, India and Pakistan, mid-1960s**

	India, 1965–6	Pakistan, 1963–4 Gross	Net[1]
	%	%	%
Plant and machinery	45	} 46	35
Agricultural machinery	25		
Basic industrial raw materials	50	} 54	33
Processed industrial materials	70		
Consumer goods	100	88	66

1. Of domestic excise and sales taxes.
Sources: Bhagwati and Desai (1970, p. 473).
Lewis (1970, p. 60).

Effective protection and commodity exchange rates

These tariff averages, or 'nominal tariffs' as they are conventionally termed today, do not permit analysis of the effects of a number of separate trade barriers upon a complex production process. Tariffs affect not only the prices of final products but also those of a wide variety of intermediate inputs. 'Industries' are therefore best thought of as processes, or activities, each of which add value to the output of the previous processes, or activities. Thus iron ore mining is one process, the manufacture of steel from the ore and other inputs is another, the manufacture of implements from the steel and other inputs is still another; the total impact of the tariff structure upon each of these processes is determined both by the trade barriers against the importation of the final output of each process and by those against the inputs to each process. The concept of 'effective protection' has been developed in order to measure the total impact of commercial and exchange rate policy upon production processes (industries).

Effective protection to industry j is defined as:

$$E_j = \frac{t_j - \overset{\Sigma}{\underset{i}{}} t_i a_{ij}}{1 - \underset{i}{\Sigma} a_{ij}} \quad \text{or} \quad \frac{t_j - \overset{\Sigma}{\underset{i}{}} t_i a_{ij},}{V_j}$$

where t_j is the rate of tariff on the final product of industry j, t_i is the rate of tariff on intermediate (non-factor) input i, a_{ij} is the free trade value of intermediate input i per unit value of the final product of industry j, and V_j is the free trade value added per unit of output in industry j. (The tariff rates must be measured net of domestic sales or excise duties.) It measures the percentage by which actual domestic value added in the industry (process) in question exceeds the value added in that industry when all inputs and the output are valued at world (free trade) prices. Thus it may also be written as $\frac{V' - V}{V}$ where V is world price value added and V' is domestic price value added. This last formulation has the virtue of permitting a more general interpretation of the concept than is suggested by the original formula which relies upon import duty rates. In many instances, import duties are not the most significant barriers to imports; physical import controls, exchange controls, multiple exchange rate systems, and inappropriately priced foreign exchange may all affect the structure of domestic prices and therefore the incentive structure with respect to various productive processes. The relevant measure in these circumstances is one which shows the effect upon domestic value added without any attempt to attribute the discrepancy between V and V' only to import duties. The former formula can be employed, of course, provided that the t's are interpreted as the difference (or, better, the expected difference) between domestic and world prices for the relevant items rather than as duty rates. The difference between domestic and world price for a particular commodity is frequently termed 'implicit protection'.

It may be worth illustrating the meaning of this measure of effective protection with a simple numerical example. Suppose that there exists an automobile assembly process which converts parts into finished vehicles in such fashion that at world, tariff-free import, prices the value of the parts amounts to 90 per cent of the value of the finished automobile; only 10 per cent of the value of the car is accounted for by value added in the assembly process. Now consider the impact of a 10 per cent import duty upon automobiles in circumstances where there exist no duties upon any of the parts. Its effect, in a small country in which import prices are given, is to raise the domestic price of the automobile by 10 per cent, but its effect upon the domestic value added is much more dramatic; with the cost of parts unchanged, value added from assembling automobiles in the country in question has risen from 10 per cent of the original price of the car to 20 per cent thereof, i.e. there has been an increase of 100 per cent in domestic value added. The rate of effective protection from a fairly modest, 10 per cent, nominal tariff is therefore seen to be 100 per cent! Had there been a simultaneous introduction of a 10 per cent import duty upon all the parts it can readily be seen that the rate of effective protection would only have been 10 per cent, the same as the nominal rate; the imposition of heavier rates of duty upon inputs than upon the final output would have produced a rate of effective protection lower than the nominal rate.

There are considerable difficulties with this apparently very useful measurement tool. Above all else, it must be recognized as a tool of partial analysis, although the use of the traditional partial geometry is not in this case especially convenient. It is employed to measure the impact of trade barriers upon particular industries or groups of industries without any allowance for indirect effects upon other industries, some of which may have feedback effects upon the industry under study. This is an extremely serious limitation, but it is no worse in this respect than alternative measures of the effect of particular tariffs. It also assumes that the intermediate input–output coefficients, the a_{ij}'s, are fixed and unaffected by the tariff; if they are, in fact, variable, the establishment of a meaningful measure of the level of effective protection becomes considerably more complex. Variation could occur either because of substitution between intermediate and factor inputs as their relative prices alter, or because of scale economies as protection-induced production expansion takes place.

If tariff rates are being employed in the measurement of effective protection rather than the world-domestic price differential, it is necessary to assume not only that tariffs are the only trade barriers, but also that the domestic price of an importable equals the world price plus tariff; this is only the case where imports for the item in question are infinitely elastic in their supply to the country in question and domestic suppliers price all the way up to the tariff. There is some evidence despite a presumption in small countries that imports are infinitely elastic in their supply, that the domestic price is often less than the world price plus tariff (King, 1970, p. 129; Bergsman, 1970, p. 41). This 'redundant protection' could be the result of competition from other similar products or of quality differentials – either real or perceived. Similarly, the use of export duties assumes that the domestic price of an export is the world price less export duty; and this is only true if the country faces an infinitely elastic world demand for that export product.

Notice that it is possible for the rate of effective protection to be negative. This can be either because the numerator in the formula is negative, in which case the process in question is, on balance, being taxed rather than protected, or because the denominator is negative, in which case the domestic production process is *so* inefficient that the value added when valued at world prices is negative, and effective protection will be less than −100 per cent. Examples of negative value added may seem unlikely, but they have been recorded in India, Pakistan and the Philippines (Little, Scitovsky and Scott, 1968, p. 186). Negative value added measurements may result from higher international transport costs for parts than for finished products, greater monopoly power on the part of foreign suppliers of parts than on that of suppliers of final products, relatively high domestic prices for non-traded inputs such as electricity or transport, artificially high intra-firm transfer prices for inputs, and failure to allow in the measurement for altered techniques in response to different input prices, as well as from sheer local inefficiencies such as high incidence of pilferage and breakage, failure to utilize waste and scrap, and severely distorted domestic prices. Negative effective protection measurements resulting from negative value added can be avoided by employing V' in the denominator of the expression for effective protection rather than V. The resulting measure of effective protection can then be interpreted as that proportion of actual value added which is attributable to protection.

Of critical importance in the establishment of meaningful measures of the incentive structure imparted to the economy by government policies in the area of foreign trade is the foreign exchange rate. More will be said about this in chapter 9 but it should be apparent already that the price at which foreign inputs or foreign outputs can be purchased is dependent not only upon tariffs and other taxes and trade barriers but also upon the price of foreign exchange, a price which may itself vary greatly from firm to firm depending upon whether the purchaser holds an import license. This is dramatically illustrated by one recent study which concludes that the long-lamented high average rates of effective protection to Latin American industry are a statistical artifact – the product of failure to allow for grossly overvalued currencies (Schydlowsky, 1970). In principle, it is desirable to ascertain the equilibrium foreign exchange rate in the absence of all controls and to calculate effective protection rates with reference to that rate.

Illustrative of the difference made by alternative measurement procedures are the data in Table 18, showing nominal and effective rates of protection, variously measured, in Pakistan. The first two columns demonstrate that the tariff is not the principal determinant of the level of protection in the majority of cases. Effective protection measurements relying only upon tariff levels diverge markedly from those which allow for the variety of other influences, such as domestic indirect taxes, the multiple exchange-rate system, and the system of quantitative controls; both the measures of effective protection differ greatly, of course, from those of nominal protection. The last four columns also demonstrate dramatically the large differences introduced to the levels of effective protection by different treatment of non-traded inputs, whether treated as inputs upon which there is no tariff or other barrier, or as part of value added. It would clearly be foolhardy to use either rankings or levels of protection, measured as described here, without a careful consideration of the methodology and its underlying assumptions.

A variant of this approach to the measurement of the structure of incentives imparted to the economy by the tariff and exchange rate policies is that of commodity or process exchange rates. Instead of calculating the percentage increase in domestic value added above free trade value added, which is made possible by these policies, one calculates the rate at which domestic currency can be exchanged for foreign currency through the domestic production of the commodity in question. Thus the commodity exchange rate for a commodity is P_d/P_f, where P_d is the commodity's domestic price in terms of home currency, and P_f is its free trade price expressed in terms of foreign currency (say \$US). As before, it is preferable to deal with processes of production rather than final products, so that the relevant expression becomes V_d/V_f, where V's refer to value added rather than to product prices, and one has 'process exchange rates' rather than commodity exchange rates. This measure is sometimes 'standardized' in terms of the official (financial) exchange rate between the currencies in question, so that the measure becomes $1/E . V_d/V_f$, where E is the official price of the foreign currency expressed in terms of the home currency. This is now very similar to the earlier expression for effective protection in which free trade value added is compared with domestic value added. Indeed, the effective rate of protection can be seen to be a standardized process exchange rate minus one.

For planning purposes, the process, or activity, exchange rate can, in principle, readily be converted into a measure of the domestic resource cost of acquiring a unit of foreign exchange in that activity by adjusting the domestic factor prices within V_d appropriately, and deducting any foreign factor earnings from V_d (and, correspondingly, V_f). In particular

Table 18 Levels of effective protection from all sources compared with levels of tariff protection only, selected industries, Pakistan, 1963–4

	Nominal tariff	% by which domestic price exceeds world price	Effective tariff protection		Effective protection from all sources	
			Non-traded inputs treated as non-deflated inputs	Non-traded inputs[1] included in value added	Non-traded inputs treated as non-deflated inputs	Non-traded inputs included in value added
	%	%	%	%	%	%
Sugar	62	215	400	133	−198	−329
Cotton textiles	159	56	−555	1900	733	213
Footwear	91	66	138	89	85	59
Plastic goods	107	236	245	170	669	335
Motor vehicles	93	249	−282	150	−164	−2100
Fertilizer	0	15	14	6	−688	186
Chemicals	33	81	13	9	300	113
Petroleum products	57	107	−49	−40	−7	−5
Cement	69	154	37	30	64	49
Non-electric machinery	12·5	89	10	8	355	170

1. Non-traded inputs can be treated either as traded inputs not subject to trade barriers, or as primary inputs to be included in value added. Levels of protection have been calculated using both methods.
Source: Lewis (1970, pp. 80–81).

observed wage rates are usually believed to exceed, and interest rates to fall short of, the resource costs to the economy of labour and capital use respectively.

It is obviously quite possible to calculate the average effective rate of protection – or the average commodity or process exchange rate – for the economy, and to compare this average over time or between countries in the same manner as was suggested for average nominal tariff rates (see, for example, Table 11). The average absolute level of effective protection is, of course, highly sensitive to the choice of exchange rate. High import duties are after all a partial alternative to devaluation.

Another calculation which can be of considerable interest, because of the general arguments for industrialization discussed above, is the average level of effective protection, or commodity exchange rate, for the *industrial* sector relative to other sectors. This has sometimes been calculated instead as an industry–agriculture commodity terms of trade, movements in which over time, particularly when considered relative to the equivalent terms of trade on world markets, trace out broad changes in government development strategy quite effectively. Greater significance is generally attached to the detailed structure of effective protection than to either global or sectoral averages, although the precise theoretical meaning to be attached to rankings, by industry, of the level of effective protection remains somewhat ambiguous.

Measurement in practice

Measurement of the structure of effective protection has burgeoned in recent years. While there have been considerable difficulties experienced in marrying the tariff classifications to the industrial classifications, acquiring suitable a_{ij}'s, devising appropriate weighting systems, determining how to deal with non-traded inputs, choosing a relevant exchange rate and measuring the differentials between world and domestic prices, enough experience has been accumulated to enable some generalizations to be made.

Effective protection is, on average, higher than nominal protection in the industrial sector both in rich countries and in poor because of the phenomenon of tariff 'cascading' or 'escalation', i.e. the general practice of levying higher import duties the higher is the degree of fabrication. The degree of dispersion of effective protection rates also generally exceeds that of nominal rates. The structure of effective protection in poor countries is such as to favour import-substituting industries relative to export processing or otherwise outward-oriented industries. (As is evident in Table 18, however, Pakistan has heavily subsidized the production of textiles which is to a significant extent an export activity; and there are such cases in other countries as well.) This bias is, of course, intensified by the industrial protection offered to their own processors by the rich nations. Within the rubric of import-substituting industry, consumer goods have received relatively far more protection than either intermediate products or capital goods in the poor countries (see Table 19). Apart from the distortion these biased incentives have created in the industrialization process, they have also, together with other factors, encouraged the unfortunate use of capital-intensive and imported input-intensive technologies throughout these economies.

As can be seen in Table 18, the rankings of industries by degree of effective protection, as well as the average levels thereof, are quite sensitive to the treatment of non-traded inputs, and to the handling of non-tariff trade barriers and domestic excise duties. Surprisingly, there is frequently a high correlation between the ranking of industries by effective tariff protection and that by nominal tariff protection; where data inadequacies do not permit the measurement of effective rates, the nominal rates may therefore provide a reasonable approximation to these rankings but this cannot, of course, be relied upon, and the tariff may not be the principal instrument of protection anyway.

For decisions as to the effects of individual tariff or other duty changes, there is still no better tool available, for all its limitations, than the effective protection measure. It can be employed for analysis of export duties as well as import duties, the former constituting a tax, i.e. a price-reducing instrument, on the

Table 19 Average effective protection rates for manufacturing, selected developing countries,[1] early 1960s

	Year	Consumption goods	Intermediate goods	Capital goods	All manufac-turing
		%	%	%	%
Argentina	1958	164	167	133	162
Brazil	1966	230	68	31	118
Mexico	1960	22	34	55	27
Pakistan	1963/4	883	88	155	271
Philippines	1965	94	65	80	49[2]

1. Calculated in relation to official exchange rates. Non-traded inputs are included in value added in all cases. For other details see original source.

2. Excluding exported manufactured goods, this figure rises to 85 per cent.

Source: Little, Scitovsky and Scott (1970, p. 174).

production of the commodity in question rather than a subsidy. Undoubtedly, more can be learnt about the impact of a tax change through the use of this concept than from the nominal change alone, however imperfect the analysis may remain. It also can offer better insights into the overall structure of incentives created by commercial policies than any other available tool. Since high effective protection can produce high profits rather than inefficiency, ranking industries by the level of effective protection cannot, however, provide a ranking as to comparative advantage.

9 Exchange Rate Policies

Discussion of commercial policies leads logically into the question of exchange rate policy. As has been seen, it is not possible to discuss the levels or the rankings of effective protection rates without taking into account the exchange rate or rates. Another way of putting this is that the total foreign exchange system is made up of a series of commodity or process exchange rates, as described in chapter 8, together with the official (financial) exchange rate or rates.

Exchange rates and exchange rate systems

The official exchange rate is declared by the Government to the International Monetary Fund and is the rate or one of the rates at which the Central Bank stands ready to transact in foreign exchange with approved participants in the foreign exchange market. It need not be an equilibrium price for foreign exchange in the sense that the market would be cleared at that price without any governmental regulation or intervention. A currency can be overvalued or undervalued by the Central Bank relative to this equilibrium rate. If the official price of foreign exchange is set at a level at which the demand of local residents, in the absence of any barriers or controls, would exceed the supply of foreign exchange to the market, the Central Bank has overvalued the domestic currency, or undervalued foreign exchange. The official rate of exchange can, in this case, be maintained either (a) by meeting the excess demand and running down the Central Bank's foreign exchange reserves or incurring further foreign debts for this purpose, or (b) by attempting to shift the demand or supply schedules through macro-economic policy or selective tax or other measures, like import tariffs or controls, or (c) by rationing out the available supply of foreign exchange to preferred customers through exchange controls, or by some combination of all three. Correspondingly, if the price of foreign exchange were set too high, and the domestic currency undervalued, in order to maintain the official rate of exchange, it would be necessary to acquire official reserves, and ease macro-economic policy, trade barriers and exchange controls. Undervaluation is much less likely to be a policy problem in developing countries.

Wherever there exist official controls over foreign exchange earnings and purchases for the sake of preserving the foreign exchange reserves at the prevailing official rate of exchange, there is bound to exist an illegal (black) market for foreign exchange in which the value of the currency in question is considerably less than the official value. The price on this illegal market is not necessarily related to the theoretical equilibrium price of foreign exchange, since it will reflect the risks of illegal activity and will portray the demand/supply position on a relatively thin and peripheral portion of the entire market.

Many governments maintain more than one exchange rate, the rate at which any particular transaction is made, depending upon the purposes of the market participant or the source of his foreign exchange earnings. The effect of such multiple exchange rates, which are enforced through a system of foreign exchange controls, is the same as a set of import and export taxes and subsidies. In some cases, official control is maintained only over certain portions of the foreign exchange market, while the remainder is left totally free to establish a market price.

Dual exchange rates are frequently recommended for developing countries as an efficient means, alternative to a tariff and subsidy scheme, of treating traditional exports subject to inelastic world demand and/or essential imports differently from other economic activities. The application of a relatively high value for the domestic currency to traditional exports and the import of essentials would tax the former and subsidize the latter. The exchange rate for the rest of the economy could easily be left, it is usually further argued, to float freely on the exchange market.

It should now be clearer than ever why import tariff protection or other trade barriers are an alternative to devaluation of the currency. Both create the same effects for the foreign exchange market disequilibrium and both create the same incentive effects upon import-competing industry. Foreign exchange controls over both current account and capital account international transactions must therefore be added to the list of policy instruments having a bearing upon the domestic incentive structure. The use of direct controls over foreign exchange transactions, like that of direct physical import controls, requires a relatively efficient and honest administrative system. It is likely to be considerably more difficult to run than a system of taxes and tariffs because of the problem of enforcement and the need to make large numbers of individual decisions about market participants.

Most developing countries have imposed exchange controls on at least some types of international transactions; to that extent most currencies in the Third World must be 'overvalued'. To describe the currency thus is not to criticize the policymakers concerned; it is a purely technical description of the fact that the official rate of exchange is not the rate at which even the tariff-adjusted demand and supply schedules would clear the foreign exchange market.

Overvalued currencies reduce the returns to exporters and to those import-competing industries or firms which are not protected by the specific exchange controls and import barriers being employed to defend the official exchange rate. In the case of exporters, they reduce the domestic currency value of foreign exchange earnings below that rate at which the market would value it, i.e. its scarcity value; in the case of import competitors, they permit the import of goods at a lower domestic currency cost than the market would call for. Whereas it has been common practice to erect import tariffs and import controls to offset the detrimental effects of overvalued currencies upon import-competing industry, there have not as frequently been analogous efforts to compensate export producers for their losses on this account. Indeed, one of the principal rationalizations of the practice of overvaluing currencies has been that by taxing export production it restricts export volume and thereby improves the terms of trade. As has been argued earlier, however, it is most unlikely that one would hope to derive improved export prices from the restriction of *all* exports, including some which have not yet been developed and may never be developed unless greater incentives are offered.

It is difficult to escape the conclusion that exchange controls and overvalued currencies were stumbled into more often than not in response to increasing balance-of-payments difficulties. It has been argued that in Latin America currency overvaluation made it feasible to subsidize the new industrial sector through taxes on the traditional export sector, in circumstances where it would have been politically impossible to impose export duties; the favoured import-substituting industrial producers were permitted to purchase their imported capital goods and intermediate inputs at the favourable overvalued rate of exchange while enjoying the protective benefits of strict controls over the importation of the final products, usually consumer goods, which they were themselves producing (Hirschman, 1968). Over-invoicing of their imported inputs and capital goods, for which there are substantial incentives wherever there exists an officially overvalued currency (Winston, 1970), probably raised these producers' profits still more. Whether this was undertaken as a matter of conscious political-economic strategy, however, is certainly open to question.

What is the 'appropriate' price for foreign exchange for purposes of planning or for the calculation of effective protection rates or possible official devaluation? As we have seen, it is that rate of exchange which would clear the foreign exchange market were government to withdraw its interventions therein. There are clearly severe conceptual problems in arriving at such a 'shadow price' for foreign exchange. Since the shadow foreign exchange rate depends upon the character of the development programme, what is to be assumed about the programme? What assumptions are to be made about the levels of tariffs, quotas, taxes and subsidies which are to be left in effect? For what time horizon is the rate to apply?

If foreign exchange revenues can be assumed to be fixed and unaffected by the choice of the exchange rate, as in the very short run and in some countries also in the medium run, they can be, and if foreign exchange reserves are reasonably stable, the appropriate equilibrium price of foreign exchange is a weighted average of the expected commodity exchange rates for all importables, where the weights are the shares of the commodities concerned in the expected or planned import bill. Those shares are themselves, in large part, determined by the elasticities of demand for individual imports. If some of the trade barriers are to be maintained following the devaluation, the relevant commodity exchange rates for the purposes of this calculation must be net of their domestic price effects. Where, however, export revenues are expected to respond to alterations in the exchange rate over the period in question, the determination of an equilibrium rate of exchange becomes rather more complex. One must then consider the domestic supply elasticities and world demand elasticities for exportables as well as demand elasticities for imports. The expected commodity exchange rates for exportables, weighted by their shares of expected total exports, must then be added into the calculation which in the simpler case relied solely upon those for importables.

The devaluation decision

Under what circumstances will it be sensible to devalue the currency, and what factors determine the outcome when a country does? Traditional analysis of currency devaluation must be carefully adapted to fit the circumstances of the typical developing country.

First of all, we must distinguish between the nominal degree of devaluation and the *effective* degree of devaluation. The frequent accompaniment of devaluation by relaxation of import quotas, exchange controls and tariffs requires that the offsetting policy alterations be netted out in order to ascertain the true or effective devaluation. Failure of a nominal devaluation to produce any effect upon the balance of payments or other targets may simply reflect the absence of any effective devaluation. Such nominal devaluations may nevertheless be useful as tidying operations which can vastly simplify the administration of commercial and exchange rate policy while leaving nearly everything else unchanged. In fact, such 'compensated devaluation' has been suggested for Latin America as a means of increasing incentives for non-traditional exports – the only sector for which the devaluation would, in this scheme, be effective – while increasing the efficiency of government (Schydlowsky, 1967).

As far as the balance-of-payments effects of an effective devaluation are concerned, it is easiest to analyse the possibilities in terms of the 'absorption' approach, rather than in that of relative prices. Apart from its theoretical complexity and the difficulty of acquiring the necessary data for its application, the relative price approach directs attention to demand and, in the complete analysis, supply elasticities which, in the short run, are unlikely to be the most crucial factors with respect to the outcome for the balance of payments. Certainly, the simple 'Marshall–Lerner condition' for balance-of-payments improvement – that the sum of the elasticities of demand for exports and for imports exceeds unity – is inapplicable because of its basic underlying assumption that supply elasticities at home as well as abroad are infinite. Even with considerable rates of overt unemployment and underemployment, the typical poor country cannot redirect its productive activity smoothly, if at all, and may be considered to be at a quasi-full employment, in that its unemployment is not the product of insufficient aggregate demand. More important, while it is likely that the elasticity (of supply as well as demand) conditions for balance-of-payments improvement through devaluation will usually be met in less developed countries, this relates only to the initial effect and does not guarantee an 'ultimately successful' devaluation.

The absorption approach portrays the import deficit $(M - X)$, i.e. imports less exports as the difference between total absorption, A, and total production, Y, where absorption is the sum of the domestic demands made by consumers, investors and government upon the current domestic total output. That is,

$M - X = A - Y.$

If, as we have suggested, there is little room for changes, at least in the short and medium run, in Y, then the import deficit will only be narrowed if there are reductions in total absorption.

Such reductions may arise from shifts in income distribution resulting from the devaluation, if these shifts are from those with higher marginal propensities to consume to those with lower ones. This is a quite likely outcome where increases in wage rates can be expected to lag behind the price increases generated by devaluation, and if profit-earners can be expected to consume less on the margin than wage-earners. Alternatively, this may result from 'money illusion' effects, if those who absorb do not perceive that their real absorption has been reduced by the price increases which result from devaluation and continue to absorb the same money values as previously; or from 'real balance' effects, if holders of monetary assets realize that their real value has been reduced by the price increases and they seek to restore them to the previous real levels by refraining from consumption. It is also possible that devaluation may decrease absorption through its effects upon prices of imports the demand for which is price-inelastic; the effect in this case is analogous to that of an excise tax which, while raising price, is deflationary in its impact.

Each of these possibilities involves reduction in aggregate demand which could produce, instead of an improved balance-of-payments position, a short-run slackening in the use of domestic productive capacity and a reduction in the level of output. This has actually been observed in Latin America (Diaz Alejandro, 1965). Since none of these effects, however, are overwhelmingly likely to be found, devaluation alone may frequently not reduce total absorption at all. It is quite possible for domestic demand to be switched, in response to the altered relative prices which are the product of devaluation, from foreign and tradeable goods and services to domestic non-tradeables without any change in total demand. In such a case, the increased demand for domestic output would generate increased imports and/or higher prices until the balance of payments returned roughly to its original state. For the desired results to be obtained, then, other policy instruments may simultaneously have to be brought to bear.

More important than the immediate balance-of-payments effects are those which manifest themselves through the supply side in longer-term alterations in the productive structure of the economy in question. Devaluation, other things being equal, alters the structure of incentives so as to encourage the domestic production of tradeable goods – exports and import-competing activities – relative to non-tradeables, or home goods, although, as has been seen, these incentive effects upon the structure of production cannot really be analysed in isolation from all of the other commercial policy influences discussed above. By shifting the economy into more productive and foreign exchange earning or saving activities over the longer run, devaluation clearly ought to ease the balance-of-payments difficulties which motivated it in the first place. If it does not achieve this shift, but merely reduces absorption, one might as well have employed deflationary macro-policies for the purpose. If, on the other hand, absorption does not fall as a result of devaluation, the restructuring of production may become quite difficult; in such circumstances, in order for devaluation to be fully effective, it may have to be accompanied by deflationary monetary and fiscal policies.

Most of the developing countries are too small to influence world prices, either for the goods and services which they import or for those which they export, regardless of the alterations in volumes of imports and exports which are the product of their devaluation. Devaluation is therefore unlikely to affect the terms of trade of the devaluing developing country unless it is a major supplier of one of the world's commodities and thus faces a world demand which is less than infinitely elastic. In the latter cases, unless the devaluation is accompanied by other measures which offset the new incentives to export, such as selective export duties upon those items which if exported in increased quantities would face lower prices, it will produce deterioration in the commodity terms of trade.

The principal reservations about the use of the tool of devaluation in the context of the developing countries have to do with its potential inflationary and income distribution effects. An effective devaluation raises the price of tradeable goods and services immediately. This increase in the price of these items may be less than proportional to the devaluation if importers lower their margins or exporters lower their foreign prices. The initial impact upon the *overall* price level will certainly be far less than proportional to the devaluation, since there exist many non-tradeable items whose prices have not immediately altered. Still, the price level will increase. The question then is what the effects of this cost-push will be upon the progress of the overall price level and upon the distribution of income. Such price increases together with those engendered by increased demand pressures upon domestic home-goods could initiate a sustained wage–price inflationary spiral.

The 'normal' pattern is for the real wage rate to fall immediately following a devaluation. Sophisticated and powerful trade unions can limit these real losses, however, by immediate wage claims. To the extent that they do, the diminished absorption which is required to improve the balance of payments is less likely to occur, except through the less plausible other effects mentioned earlier. The outcome will therefore probably be an overall wage and price increase which offsets the devaluation, leaving the incentive structure, the level of absorption and the balance of payments essentially unaltered. (There is some risk, as has already been suggested, that the inflation could acquire a momentum of its own and overshoot the balance-of-payments position at which the process began.) Inflation carries with it further distributional effects which also have to be considered in the analysis of the ultimate impact of the devaluation.

Only if the government has the power and the determination to hold the wage and price line, through firm monetary and fiscal action, can devaluation be sure to escape these pitfalls; it may then, however, find itself generating unemployment instead. The likelihood of an inflationary outcome is obviously reduced if the devaluation happens to be accompanied by a good food crop and stable or falling food prices which could leave real wage rates essentially unaltered despite the increased prices of tradeable goods.

It should by now be clear that there are important income distribution implications in the apparently neutral instrument of devaluation. Urban wage earners, particularly those who consume imported goods in large quantities, can be expected to oppose effective devaluation vigorously as a device to lower their real wages. Any other groups with fixed incomes or the prospect of lagging adjustment to increases in the cost of living can also be expected to oppose it. Exporters, who in some cases are the major landowners, are the principal sufferers from an overvalued currency and they can be expected to press for and welcome a devaluation; so can the owners of capital and managers in the unprotected portions of the import-substituting industrial sector. It is small wonder, then, that recourse to devaluation has been regarded by many, particularly in Latin America, as a conservative response to economic difficulties. Needless to say, the distributional component is not the only part of the complex policy equation; however, it is obviously one which carries great political weight.

10 Economic Integration

The absence of strong trade ties among the developing countries (see Table 20) is not solely due to trade barriers; one would not therefore expect their removal necessarily to generate a burst of trade among members of an integration scheme. Inadequate and costly transport facilities, coupled sometimes with freight rates which discriminate against trade among developing countries, also constitute important barriers to trade. Even within these nations, transport facilities are typically far more geared to the movement of primary produce to ports for shipment abroad than to internal trade. Financing facilities for international trade are also much more developed along the traditional trade routes to the metropolitan centres than they are in the 'newer' spheres of internal trade or trade among developing countries. In any case, the economies of adjoining poor countries are likely to be engaged in the same sort of exporting activity; only as they begin to develop more diversified structures of production are they likely to be able to exchange large quantities to

Table 20 **Exports of less developed countries to other less developed countries as a percentage of their total exports, 1965 and 1969**

	1965	1969
	%	%
Latin America	19·3	20·7
Developing Africa	11·9	10·1
Asian Middle East	20·6	20·5
Other Asia	31·2	31·8
Total	21·0	20·6

Source: Calculated from UN, *Monthly Bulletin of Statistics.*

their mutual advantage. Whether they actually do so or not will depend upon the degree to which there is co-ordination of development programmes and freedom from trade barriers between them as they develop.

One instrument of industrialization and development strategy, and of tariff and commercial policy, which is universally recommended to, and in principle approved of by, the developing countries is the formation of customs unions, free trade areas and common markets. There exist many other forms of economic co-operation which are also desirable, such as payments unions; common transport, communications, research and other service institutions; co-ordinated river basin development plans; regional development banks; commodity marketing schemes, etc. None of these have as yet, however, attracted the attention of the economist or policymaker to the extent that common tariff arrangements have. Particularly has this been so in the last decade when the example of the European Economic Community has inspired efforts to replicate its success elsewhere. Under the terms of the GATT only one type of preferential tariff reduction is permitted – that being a 100 per cent preference in which duties are completely removed with respect to the partner states. States which discriminate in one another's favour in this manner, however, are not required to unify their tariffs with respect to the non-members. If they do so, they are said to be forming a 'customs union', and if not, they are forming a 'free trade area'. (A 'common market' is a customs union in which labour and capital as well as goods are allowed to flow freely among the partner states.)

The core of the theory of customs unions as developed in the context of the Western European experience is not particularly useful for the analysis of economic integration schemes in most of the developing countries because of its focus upon the static allocation effects within flexible industrialized economies. As will be seen, it may be applicable to some of the integration schemes in Latin America. For the present, however, it will be more useful to place heaviest emphasis upon the aspects of the theory which are most relevant to the context of the majority of developing countries.

The essence of the case for economic integration in the developing areas is the need to take advantage of economies of scale in industries which have not yet been established. Import-substituting industrialization is under way throughout the poor nations for various reasons and under varying levels of protection. Given this fact, and the small size of the typical national market, there is obviously a lot to be gained through co-ordination of industrial planning so as to avoid unnecessary duplication which would produce sub-optimal scale, under-utilization and inefficiencies. Integration schemes in the developing countries are thus best thought of as co-operative protection schemes against non-members within which industrial markets are 'swapped' in such a manner that the aggregate import substitution programme is attained at lower total cost, and with a greater degree of specialization, than if each member had proceeded with its own programme independently. In terms of static customs union theory, this market-swapping constitutes 'trade diversion' which is not in the world interest or in that of the member-states, because it diverts trade from a low-cost source outside the membership to a higher-cost source within it; but if the diversion were otherwise to occur anyway through protection of each independent national industrial sector against other industrial nations, the co-ordination of industrial protection is a desirable second-best, even in terms of this theory, as long as there exist any scale economies.

From this approach to integration the corollary follows that the removal of barriers to trade among the member-states is a necessary but not a sufficient condition for attaining the benefits of co-ordinated industrialization. Unless it is accompanied by co-ordinated industrial planning, at least for those industries in which scale economies are believed to exist, it will be to no avail. One does not have to look far for examples to illustrate this point; many states or provinces, particularly those within weak federations, do not even reap the full potential benefits of membership in the 'common market' of their own country. The difficulty of reaching agreement on the location of Nigeria's iron and steel complex springs to mind.

In instances where, as in some countries in Latin America,

there is already a considerable industrial sector, economic integration may, without planning, induce rationalization of industry which is already in existence, simply through the discipline of the market-place. This need not involve the shutdown of less efficient plants; it can instead be achieved through intra-product specialization in which each firm or plant in the industry engages more intensively in the production of differentiated sub-products rather than in the production of the whole range of the industry's output. In terms of customs union theory, 'trade creation' may, in these instances, also take place – the shift of production from a domestic high-cost source to a foreign lower-cost source. (It is possible that there exist still lower-cost sources outside the membership in which case there could be even more 'trade creation' through a move to free trade with respect to everyone, instead of only discriminatorily with respect to one's partners.) As in the case of potential scale economies, this rationalization will raise the efficiency of the members' joint industrial programme. It is hoped that the new Andean Common Market will create 'orthodox' gains of this sort. 'Trade creation' may also, of course, occur in agricultural products.

There exist other rationales for economic integration arrangements in the developing countries, but they are all of secondary importance. For instance, if the bloc of states forming an agreement is large enough, it may extract improvements in the terms of trade with respect to non-members by offering, as a bloc, a reduced supply of exports and a reduced demand for imports to the rest of the world. In the same vein, a large bloc can presumably carry greater weight in international negotiations over tariffs and trade than could the sum of its members acting independently. It is also frequently claimed that the creation of large industrial markets will generate more external economies and/or attract more foreign investment. Both of these claims may be correct, but they are the outcome of the emergence of the opportunity for realizing scale economies in the industrialization process rather than separate arguments for economic integration; without scale economies these possibilities fall to the ground. A further argument pointing to the advantages of export diversification for the members is again not so much an argument for integration as for structural change and/or the formation of foreign exchange reserve pools.

The advantages of economic integration agreements among developing nations are so obvious and are paid such extravagant lip-service that one finds oneself wondering why successful agreements of this kind have been so few. A great many common markets, customs unions and free trade areas have been formed on paper, only to die slowly later as the details fail to be negotiated to all the members' satisfaction. The central problem is the creation of an agreement which not only avoids penalizing any of the members for membership but also distributes the gains therefrom reasonably equitably.

In the first place, an agreement to remove tariffs against the products of a partner, while continuing, jointly, to impose protective duties on those products with respect to non-members, will result in a nation's imposing higher import prices upon itself. As long as the protection against non-members is effective, the country removing duties *vis-à-vis* its partner will pay the protected price – world price plus tariff – for its imports from the partner when it formerly obtained them at the (lower) world price. The government budget will feel this cost directly in the form of the disappearance of the import duty revenues it formerly collected upon the imports in question. A nation will presumably only agree to increase the cost of its imports in this way if it receives better prices for its exports to the partner or some other form of compensation in return. If there exists one member with a relatively well-developed industrial sector, it may be difficult to avoid imposing worsened terms of trade upon the less developed members through their participation.

Apart from the possibility of such internal terms of trade effects, there may also be a tendency for all the industrial activity to concentrate around the original industrial base, since that is where the industrial infrastructure and other external benefits thrown off by the 'pole' can best be realized. The polarization of industrial activity in one country can create 'backwash' effects for the others, with capital, skilled labour and entrepreneurship in other parts of the tariff-free area all gravitating to the growth pole, at the expense of the potential growth of the areas from which they came. While the growth of the pole could create 'spillover' effects upon the remainder, these will be substantially offset by the increasing terms of trade effects mentioned above.

These factors suggest that it will be easiest to negotiate functioning integration agreements where all of the members are at about the same level of industrial development and are of about the same economic size. If there are severe imbalances at the outset, the difficulty of working out some means of satisfying the least developed members that their development will not suffer as a consequence of membership greatly reduces the chances of success.

Various devices have been attempted as solutions to this problem of equitable distribution of benefits and costs. One possibility is to offer direct financial transfers to the governments of the weaker members – either as lump sums or on the basis of formulae applied to the distribution of customs revenues or the financing or functioning of common development institutions. This solution was employed within the East African Common Market in the early 1960s. If, however, the policymakers in the weaker members have industrialization in their objective functions, rather than merely national income, even heavy compensating payments may not satisfy them for their failure to have their own industries. In this case it may be necessary to work out a scheme which discriminates in favour of the industrial development of the least developed members through tax incentives, delayed introduction of tariff reductions, subsidy arrangements and/or discretionary action on the part of a common industrial licensing authority.

It may be worth mentioning at least two such arrangements for the promotion of industrial balance, one in the Central American Common Market and the other in the East African Community. In the CACM, the treaty provided for the designation of particular industries within which scale economies could be expected as 'integration industries'. Once so designated, trade in their products was immediately to be freed from all restrictions; there was presumably not intended to be more than one plant permitted by the licensing authority for each such industry within the Common Market. No member was to receive two integration industries before each member had received one. The complexity of the designation procedures has slowed the scheme, but it has enabled one or two 'regional' industries to be established within the common market in a more balanced fashion than would otherwise have occurred. (This balance may have been attained at the cost of some efficiency.)

In the more recent Treaty for East African Co-operation, provision is made for countries in deficit on manufactured-goods trade with respect to the other members to impose 'transfer taxes', a euphemism for import duties, against their partners up to certain stipulated limits and stipulated maximum periods of time. Tanzania has employed them to build up its own industrial base at the expense of Kenyan exports to Tanzania. Unfortunately, there is no detailed provision in this treaty for regional co-ordination of industrial planning. In both the Central American and the East African cases, however, the common development banks are emerging as potentially important promoters of regional industrial planning for the realization of the maximum scale economies consistent with the desired industrial balance.

One device to free the least developed at least from the potential losses on account of terms of trade deterioration is the negotiation of a free trade area instead of a common market or customs union. If a country then considers the cost of protecting a partner state's industry as too high, it can reduce its tariff with respect to third countries on its own and shift its purchases back to the lowest-cost source. If this is done, however, some of the rationale is lost for creating the integration scheme in the first place, which was to build a co-ordinated industrial import-substitution programme.

It is possible, however, to negotiate the swapping of national markets on an industry-by-industry basis from the base of a free trade area; and this is indeed what occurred, through so-called 'complementarity agreements' within the Latin American Free Trade Area, which did not function very effectively on other counts. It would probably be possible to negotiate industry-by-industry agreements for tariff removal even without the rubric of a free trade area, and to obtain exemptions from the GATT terms if it were felt necessary to legalize them. It is possible that more progress will be achieved, in future, through detailed negotiation of industry-specific co-ordinated development plans and trading arrangements, rather than by attempting to leap directly to fully generalized customs unions, the experience with which in most of Asia, Africa and Latin America has not so far been very encouraging.

References

ADAMS, N. A. (1967), 'Import structure and economic growth: a comparison of cross-section and time series data', *Economic Development and Cultural Change*, vol. 15, no. 2, pt. 1, pp. 143–62.

ALLEN, R. L. (1961), 'Integration in less developed areas', *Kyklos*, vol. 14, fasc. 3, pp. 315–36.

AMIN, S. (1971), 'Development and structural changes: African experience', in B. Ward, J. D. Runnalls, and L. D'Anjou (eds.), *The Widening Gap: Development in the 1970s*, Colombia University Press, pp. 312–33.

ARGY, V. (1970), 'Structural inflation in developing countries', *Oxford Economic Papers*, vol. 22, no. 1, pp. 73–85.

BACHA, E., and TAYLOR, L. (1971), 'Foreign exchange shadow prices: a critical review of current theories', *Quarterly Journal of Economics*, vol. 85, no. 2, pp. 197–224.

BAER, W. (1962), *The Puerto Rican Economy and United States Economic Fluctuations*, Social Science Research Center, University of Puerto Rico.

BAER, W. (1969), *The Development of the Brazilian Steel Industry*, Vanderbilt.

BALASSA, B. (1967), 'The impact of the industrial countries' tariff structure on their imports of manufactures from less-developed areas', *Economica*, vol. 34, no. 136, pp. 372–83.

BALASSA, B. (1969), 'Country size and trade patterns: comment', *American Economic Review*, vol. 59, no. 1, pp. 201–4.

BALASSA, B. (1971a), *The Structure of Protection in Developing Countries*, Johns Hopkins.

BALASSA, B. (1971b), 'Trade policies in developing countries', *American Economic Review*, vol. 61, no. 2, pp. 178–87.

BALASSA, B., GUISINGER, S. E., and SCHYDLOWSKY, D. M. (1970), 'The effective rates of protection and the question of labor protection in the United States: a comment', *Journal of Political Economy*, vol. 78, no. 5, pp. 1150–62.

BALASSA, B. and SCHYDLOWSKI, D. M. (1968), 'Effective tariffs, domestic cost of foreign exchange, and the equilibrium rate', *Journal of Political Economy*, vol. 76, no. 3, pp. 348–60.

BALDWIN, R. E. (1961), 'Exchange rate policy and economic development', *Economic Development and Cultural Change*, vol. 9, no. 4, pt. 1, pp. 598–603.

BALDWIN, R. E. (1963), 'Export technology and development from a subsistence level', *Economic Journal*, vol. 73, no. 289, pp. 80–92.

BARAN, P. (1957), *The Political Economy of Growth*, Monthly Review Press.

BERGSMAN, J. (1970), *Brazil, Industrialization and Trade Policies*, Development Centre, OECD, Oxford University Press.

BHAGWATI, J. N., and DESAI, P. (1970), *India, Planning for Industrialization: Industrialization and Trade Policies Since 1951*, Development Centre, OECD, Oxford University Press.

BRAINARD, W. C., and COOPER, R. N. (1968), 'Uncertainty and diversification in international trade', *Food Research Institute Studies in Agricultural Economics, Trade and Development*, vol. 8, no. 3, pp. 257–85, Stanford University.

BRUNO, M. (1967), 'The optimal selection of export-promoting and import-substituting projects', in *Planning the External Sector: Techniques, Problems, Policies*, United Nations, pp. 88–135.

BRUTON, H. J. (1969), 'The two-gap approach to aid and development', *American Economic Review*, vol. 59, no. 3; and 'Reply' by H. B. Chenery, pp. 439–49.

BRUTON, H. J. (1970), 'The import-substitution strategy of economic development: a survey', *Pakistan Development Review*, vol. 10, no. 2, pp. 123–46.

CAINE, S. (1954), 'Instability of primary product prices – a protest and a proposal', *Economic Journal*, vol. 64, no. 255, pp. 610–14.

CHENERY, H. B. (1960), 'Patterns of industrial growth', *American Economic Review*, vol. 50, no. 4, pp. 624–54.

CHENERY, H. B. (1961), 'Comparative advantage and development policy', *American Economic Review*, vol. 51, no. 1, pp. 18–51.

CHENERY, H. B. (1971), 'Targets for development', in B. Ward, J. D. Runnalls and L. D'Anjou (eds.), *The Widening Gap: Development in the 1970s*, Columbia University Press, pp. 27–47.

CHENERY, H. B. and STROUT, A. M. (1966), 'Foreign assistance and economic development', *American Economic Review*, vol. 56, no. 4, pt. 1, pp. 679–733.

CHENERY, H. B., and TAYLOR, L. (1968), 'Development patterns among countries and over time', *Review of Economics and Statistics*, vol. 50, no. 4, pp. 391–416.

CLARK, P. B. (1970), *Planning Import Substitution*, North-Holland.

COHEN, B. (1968), 'The less-developed countries' exports of primary products', *Economic Journal*, vol. 78, no. 310, pp. 334–43.

COHEN, B. I. (1971), 'The use of effective tariffs', *Journal of Political Economy*, vol. 79, no. 1, pp. 128–41.

COHEN, B. I., and SISLER, D. G. (1970), *Exports of Developing Countries in the 1960s*, Economic Growth Centre, Yale University, Discussion Paper no. 86.

COOPER, C. A., and MASSELL, B. F. (1965), 'Toward a general theory of customs unions for developing countries', *Journal of Political Economy*, vol. 73, no. 5, pp. 461–76.

COOPER, R. N. (1971a), 'Currency devaluation in developing countries', in G. Ranis (ed.), *Government and Economic Development*, Yale University Press, pp. 472–512.

COOPER, R. N. (1971b), 'Devaluation and aggregate demand in aid-receiving countries', in J. N. Bhagwati, R. W. Jones, R. A. Mundell and J. Vanek (eds.), *Trade, Balance of Payments and Growth: Papers in International Economics in Honor of Charles P. Kindleberger*, North-Holland, pp. 355–76.

COPPOCK, J. D. (1962), *International Economic Instability*, McGraw-Hill.

CORDEN, W. M. (1966), 'The structure of a tariff system and the effective protective rate', *Journal of Political Economy*, vol. 74, no. 3, pp. 221–37.

DE VRIES, B. A. (1967), 'Export experiences of developing countries', *World Bank Staff Occasional Papers*, no. 3, Johns Hopkins.

DE VRIES, M. G. (1966). 'Trade and exchange policy and economic development: two decades of evolving views', *Oxford Economic Papers*, vol. 18, no. 1.

DIAZ ALEJANDRO, C. F. (1965), *Exchange-Rate Devaluation in a Semi-Industrialized Country*, MIT.

DIAZ ALEJANDRO, C. F. (1970), *Essays on the Economic History of the Argentine Republic*, Yale University Press.

EMERY, R. F. (1967), 'The relation of exports to economic growth', *Kyklos*, vol. 20, fasc. 2, pp. 470–86.

ERB, G. F., and SCHIAVO-CAMPO, S. (1969), 'Export instability, level of development, and economic size of less-developed countries', *Bulletin of the Oxford University Institute of Economics and Statistics*, vol. 31, no. 4, pp. 263–83.

GLASSBURNER, B. (1968), 'Aspects of the problem of foreign exchange pricing in Pakistan', *Economic Development and Cultural Change*, vol. 16, no. 4, pp. 517–38.

GOODE, R., LENT, G. E., and OJHA, P. D. (1966), 'Role of export taxes in developing countries', *IMF Staff Papers*, vol. 13, pp. 453–503.

GREEN, R. H. (1971), 'Political independence and the national economy: an essay on the political economy of decolonization', in C. Allen and R. W. Johnson (eds.), *African Perspectives: Papers in the History, Politics and Economics of Africa presented to Thomas Hodgkin*, Cambridge University Press.

HAGEN, E. E. (1958), 'An economic justification of protectionism', *Quarterly Journal of Economics*, vol. 72, no. 4, pp. 496–514.

HELLEINER, G. K. (1966), *Peasant Agriculture, Government and Economic Growth in Nigeria*, Irwin.

HINRICHS, H. H. (1965), 'Determinants of government revenue shares among less-developed countries', *Economic Journal*, vol. 75, no. 299, pp. 546–56.

HIRSCHMAN, A. O. (1968), 'The political economy of import-substituting industrialization in Latin America', *Quarterly Journal of Economics*, vol. 82, no. 1, pp. 1–32.

HSING, M.-H. (1971), *Taiwan: Industrialization and Trade Policies*, Development Centre, OECD, Oxford University Press; under same cover as Power and Sicat (1971).

INTERNATIONAL MONETARY FUND, *International Financial Statistics*, IMF.

INTERNATIONAL MONETARY FUND–INTERNATIONAL BANK FOR RECONSTRUCTION AND DEVELOPMENT (1969), *The Problem of Stabilization of Prices of Primary Products*, IMF.

JOHNSON, H. G. (1964), 'Tariffs and economic development', *Journal of Development Studies*, vol. 1, no. 1, pp. 3–30.

JOHNSON, H. G. (1965), 'A theoretical model of economic nationalism in new and developing states', *Political Science Quarterly*, vol. 80, no. 2, pp. 169–85.

JOHNSON, H. G. (1967), *Economic Policies Toward Less Developed Countries*, Brookings Institution.

KALDOR, N. (1964), 'Dual exchange rates and economic development', UN Economic Commission for Latin America, *Economic Bulletin for Latin America*, vol. 9, no. 2, pp. 215–23.

KEESING, D. B. (1967), 'Outward-looking policies and economic development', *Economic Journal*, vol. 77, no. 306, pp. 303–20.

KILBY, P. (1969), *Industrialization in an Open Economy: Nigeria, 1945–66*, Cambridge University Press.

KINDLEBERGER, C. P. (1968), 'Disequilibrium systems of foreign trade and the developing countries', in J. D. Theberge (ed.), *Economics of Trade and Development*, Wiley, pp. 490–505.

KING, T. (1970), *Mexico: Industrialization and Trade Policies Since 1940*, Development Centre, OECD, Oxford University Press.

KRAVIS, I. B. (1968), 'International commodity agreements to promote aid and efficiency: the case of coffee', *Canadian Journal of Economics*, vol. 1, no. 2, pp. 295–317.

KRAVIS, I. B. (1970), 'External demand and internal supply factors in LDC export performance', *Banca Nazionale del Lavoro Quarterly Review*, vol. 23, no. 93, pp. 157–79.

KRUEGER, A. O. (1966), 'Some economic costs of exchange control: the Turkish case', *Journal of Political Economy*, vol. 74, no. 5, pp. 466–80.

KUZNETS, S. (1964), 'Quantitative aspects of the economic growth of nations: IX. Level and structure of foreign trade: comparisons for recent years', *Economic Development and Cultural Change*, vol. 13, no. 1, pt. 2.

KUZNETS, S. (1967), 'Quantitative aspects of the economic growth of nations: X. Level and structure of foreign trade: long-term trends', *Economic Development and Cultural Change*, vol. 15, no. 2, pt. 2.

LARY, H. B. (1968), *Imports of Manufactures from Less-Developed Countries*, National Bureau of Economic Research.

LEFF, N. H. (1968), *The Brazilian Capital Goods Industry, 1929–64*, Harvard University Press.

LEFF, N. H. (1969), 'The "exportable surplus" approach to foreign trade, underdeveloped countries', *Economic Development and Cultural Change*, vol. 17, no. 3, pp. 346–55.

LEVIN, J. V. (1960), *The Export Economies*, Harvard University Press.

LEWIS, S. R. (1968), 'Effects of trade policy on domestic relative prices: Pakistan 1951–64', *American Economic Review*, vol. 58, no. 1, pp. 60–78.

LEWIS, S. R. (1970), *Pakistan: Industrialization and Trade Policies*, Development Centre, OECD, Oxford University Press.

LEWIS, S. R. and GUISINGER, S. E. (1968), 'Measuring protection in a developing country: the case of Pakistan', *Journal of Political Economy*, vol. 76, no. 6, pp. 1170–98.

LEWIS, W. A. (1969), *Aspects of Tropical Trade, 1883–1965*, the Wicksell Lectures, 1969, Almqvist and Wicksell.

LINDER, S. B. (1961), *An Essay on Trade and Transformation*, Almqvist and Wicksell.

LITTLE, I., SCITOVSKY, T., and SCOTT, M. (1970), *Industry and Trade in Some Developing Countries: A Comparative Study*, Development Centre, OECD, Oxford University Press.

MACARIO, S. (1964), 'Protectionism and industrialization in Latin America', UN Economic Commission for Latin America, *Economic Bulletin for Latin America*, vol. 9, no. 1, pp. 61–101.

MACBEAN, A. I. (1966), *Export Instability and Economic Development*, Harvard University Press.

MAIZELS, A. (1963), *Industrial Growth and World Trade*, Cambridge University Press.

MAIZELS, A. (1968), *Exports and Economic Growth of Developing Countries*, Cambridge University Press.

MALMGREN, H. B. (1971), *Trade for Development*, Overseas Development Council.

MASSELL, B. F. (1964), 'Export concentration and fluctuations in export earnings: a cross-section analysis', *American Economic Review*, vol. 54, no. 2, pt. 1, pp. 47–63.

MASSELL, B. F. (1970), 'Export instability and economic structure', *American Economic Review*, vol. 60, no. 4, pp. 618–30.

McKINNON, R. (1964), 'Foreign exchange constraints in economic development and efficient aid allocation', *Economic Journal*, vol. 74, no. 294, pp. 388–409.

MEAD, D. C. (1966), *Growth and Structural Change in the Egyptian Economy*, Irwin.

MEAD, D. C. (1968), 'The distribution of gains in customs unions between developing countries', *Kyklos*, vol. 21, fasc. 4, pp. 713–36.

MEIER, G. M. (1968), *The International Economics of Development*, Harper & Row.

MICHAELY, M. (1962), *Concentration in International Trade*, North-Holland.

MIKESELL, R. F. (1963), 'The theory of common markets as applied to regional arrangements among developing countries', in R. Harrod and D. Hague (eds.), *International Trade Theory in a Developing World*, Macmillan, ch. 9, pp. 205–29.

MIKESELL, R. F., *et al.* (1971), *Foreign Investment in the Petroleum and Mineral Industries*, Resources for the Future, Johns Hopkins.

MILES, C. (1964), 'The market for manufactures of underdeveloped countries', in *New Directions for World Trade*, Royal Institute for International Affairs, Oxford University Press, pp. 115–38.

MIRRLEES, J. A. (1971), 'The terms of trade: Pearson on trade policy, debt and liquidity', in B. Ward, J. D. Runnalls and L. D'Anjou (eds.), *The Widening Gap: Development in the 1970s*, Columbia University Press, pp. 165–85.

MORLEY, S. A., and SMITH, G. W. (1970), 'On the measurement of import substitution', *American Economic Review*, vol. 60, no. 4, pp. 728–35.

MYINT, H. (1963), 'Infant industry arguments for assistance to industries in the setting of dynamic trade theory', in R. Harrod and D. Hague (eds.), *International Trade Theory in a Developing World*, Macmillan, ch. 7, pp. 173–94.

MYINT, H. (1967), 'The inward- and outward-looking countries of southeast Asia', *Malayan Economic Review*, vol. 12, no. 1, pp. 1–13.

MYINT, H. (1969), 'International trade and the developing countries', in P. A. Samuelson (ed.), *International Economic Relations*, Macmillan and St Martin's Press, pp. 15–35.

NIGERIAN INSTITUTE OF SOCIAL AND ECONOMIC RESEARCH (1969), *Conference on National Reconstruction and Development: Economic and Social Survey*, Ibadan.

PACK, H., and TODARO, M. (1969), 'Technological transfer, labour absorption and economic development', *Oxford Economic Papers*, vol. 21, no. 3, pp. 395–403.

PAPANEK, G. F. (ed.) (1968), *Development Policy: Theory and Practice*, Harvard University Press, chs. 4–7.

PEARSON, L. B. *et al.* (1969), *Partners in Development: Report of the Commission on International Development*, Praeger.

PINCUS, J. (1967), *Trade, Aid and Development: The Rich and Poor Nations*, McGraw-Hill.

PORTER, R. C. (1970), 'Some implications of post-war primary-product trends', *Journal of Political Economy*, vol. 78, no. 3, pp. 586–97.

POWER, J. H. (1966), 'Import substitution as an industrialization strategy', *Philippine Economic Journal*, no. 10, second semester, vol. 5, no. 2, pp. 167–204.

POWER, J. H., and SICAT, G. P. (1971), *The Philippines: Industrialization and Trade Policies*, Development Centre, OECD, Oxford University Press; under same cover as Hsing (1971).

PREBISCH, R. (1959), 'Commercial policy in the underdeveloped countries', *American Economic Review*, vol. 49, no. 2, pp. 215–73.

PROCEEDINGS OF THE UNITED NATIONS CONFERENCE ON TRADE AND DEVELOPMENT (1964), First Session, Geneva.

PROCEEDINGS OF THE UNITED NATIONS CONFERENCE ON TRADE AND DEVELOPMENT (1968a), Second Session, vol. 2, *Commodity Problems and Policies*, New Delhi, UN.

PROCEEDINGS OF THE UNITED NATIONS CONFERENCE ON TRADE AND DEVELOPMENT (1968b), Second Session, vol. 3, *Problems and Policies of Trade in Manufactures and Semi-Manufactures*, New Delhi, UN.

RAQUIBUZZAMAN, M. (1970), 'The economic implications of complete free trade and an alternative form of free trade in sugar through 1980', *Pakistan Development Review*, vol. 10, no. 3, pp. 334–58.

REYNOLDS, C. W. (1963), 'Domestic consequences of export instability', *American Economic Review*, vol. 53, no. 2, pp. 93–102.

ROBSON, P. (1968), *Economic Integration in Africa*, Allen & Unwin.

ROE, A. R. (1969), 'Terms of trade and transfer effects in the East African Common Market', *Bulletin of the Oxford University Institute of Economics and Statistics*, vol. 31, no. 3, pp. 153–67.

ROJKO, A. S., and MACKIE, A. B. (1970), 'World demand prospects for agricultural exports of less-developed countries in 1980', *Foreign Agricultural Economic Report*, no. 60, US Dept. of Agriculture, Economic Research Service.

ROWE, J. W. F. (1965), *Primary Commodities in International Trade*, Cambridge University Press.

ROZEN, M. E. (1969), 'Some observations on the efficiency of industrialization', *Pakistan Development Review*, vol. 9, no. 4, pp. 357–79.

SCHIAVO-CAMPO, S. (1968), 'Supplementary financing: the proposals and the issues', *Food Research Institute Studies in Agricultural Economics, Trade and Development*, Stanford University, vol. 8, no. 2, pp. 137–54.

SCHYDLOWSKY, D. M. (1967), 'Analytical basis for a national policy on regional economic integration in Latin America', *Journal of Common Market Studies*, vol. 6, no. 2, pp. 179–95.

SCHYDLOWSKY, D. M. (1967), 'From import substitution to export promotion for semi-grown-up industries: a policy proposal', *Journal of Development Studies*, vol. 3, no. 4, pp. 405–13.

SCHYDLOWSKY, D. M. (1970), *Latin American Trade Policies in the 1970s: A Prospective Appraisal*, prepared for the Columbia University Conference on International Economic Development, Pearson Conference Document no. 24, unpublished.

SCITOVSKY, T. (1960), 'International trade and economic integration as a means of overcoming the disadvantages of a small nation', in E. A. G. Robinson (ed.), *Economic Consequences of the Size of Nations*, Macmillan and St Martin's Press, pp. 282–90.

SEERS, D. (1959), 'An approach to the short-period analysis of primary producing economies', *Oxford Economic Papers*, vol. 11, no. 1, pp. 1–36.

SEERS, D. (1963), 'The stages of economic development of a primary producer in the middle of the twentieth century', *Economic Bulletin of Ghana*, vol. 7, no. 4, pp. 57–69.

SEERS, D. (1964), 'The mechanism of an open petroleum economy', *Social and Economic Studies*, vol. 13, no. 2, pp. 233–42.

SICAT, G. P (1969), *Economic Progress in South Korea and Taiwan: Lessons for the Philippines*, Institute of Economic Development and Research, University of the Philippines, Discussion Paper no. 69–17.

SOLIGO, R. (1971), 'Real and illusory aspects of an overvalued exchange rate: the Pakistan case', *Oxford Economic Papers*, vol. 23, no. 1, pp. 90–109.

STREETEN, P. (1969), 'The case for export subsidies', *Journal of Development Studies*, vol. 5, no. 4, pp. 270–73.

SYMPOSIUM 1 (1958), 'The quest for a stabilization policy in primary producing countries', *Kyklos*, vol. 11, fasc. 1, pp. 139–265.

SYMPOSIUM 2 (1959), 'Stabilization and development in primary producing countries', *Kyklos*, vol. 12, fasc. 2, pp. 269–401.

THEBERGE, J. D. (ed.) (1968), *Economics of Trade and Development*, Wiley.

UNITED NATIONS (1952), *Instability in Export Markets of Underdeveloped Countries*, Dept. of Economic Affairs.

UNITED NATIONS (1967), 'Trade expansion and economic

co-operation among developing countries', *Journal of Common Market Studies*, vol. 6, no. 3, pp. 88–115.

UNITED NATIONS CONFERENCE ON TRADE AND DEVELOPMENT (1967), *Trade Expansion and Economic Integration Among Developing Countries*, UN.

UNITED NATIONS CONFERENCE ON TRADE AND DEVELOPMENT (1969), *Review of International Trade and Development*, UN.

UNITED REPUBLIC OF TANZANIA (1970), *The Economic Survey and Annual Plan 1970–71*, Tanzania.

WALTER, I. (1971), 'Non-tariff barriers and the export performance of developing economies', *American Economic Review*, vol. 61, no. 2, pp. 195–205.

WARD, B., RUNNALLS, J. D., and D'ANJOU, L. (eds.) (1971), *The Widening Gap: Development in the 1970s*, Columbia University Press.

WATKINS, M. H. (1963), 'A staple theory of economic growth', *Canadian Journal of Economics and Political Science*, vol. 29, no. 2, pp. 141–58.

WINSTON, G. C. (1970), 'Over-invoicing, under-utilization and distorted industrial growth', *Pakistan Development Review*, vol. 10, no. 4, pp. 405–21.

WIONCZEK, M. S. (ed.) (1966), *Latin American Economic Integration: Experiences and Prospects*, Praeger.

ZANDANO, G. (1969), 'The Heckscher–Ohlin model and the tariff structures of the industrial countries', *Banca Nazionale del Lavoro Quarterly Review*, vol. 22, no. 88, pp. 46–65.

Index

Penguin Modern Economics Texts

A new series of short, original unit texts on various aspects of thought and research in important areas of economics. The series is under the general editorship of B. J. McCormick, Senior Lecturer in Economics, University of Sheffield.

Analytical Welfare Economics
D. M. Winch

Balance-of-Payments Policy
B. J. Cohen

Consumer Theory
H. A. John Green

The Control of the Money Supply
A. D. Bain

The Economics of Agriculture
David Metcalf

The Economics of the Common Market
D. Swann

Elements of Regional Economics
Harry W. Richardson

Household Behaviour
M. Bruce Johnson

Industrial Concentration
M. A. Utton